SHORT CIRCUIT TO GOD
The Electrifying Spiritual Journey of Frank Kelly

David P. Lang

FB
Francis Books • Marshfield, Massachusetts

Short Circuit to God
The Electrifying Spiritual Journey of Frank Kelly
By David P. Lang

Published by:
Francis Books

Francis B. Kelly
P.O. Box 81
Humarock, MA 02047

Website: www.frankkelly.org

ISBN: 0-9729878-0-0

First printing 2003
Second printing 2004
Third printing 2005
Fourth printing 2007
Fifth printing 2008 (Jan.)
Sixth printing 2008 (Nov.)
Seventh printing 2009
Eighth printing 2010
Ninth printing 2012
Tenth printing 2013
Eleventh printing 2016

Printed in the United States of America

Cover design by Ahrens Design, Franklin, Massachusetts
Front cover photograph of Frank Kelly's hand with Rosary
    by Dave Lang

Imprimatur: Most Rev. John Mulagada, D.D.
            Bishop, Diocese of Eluru, India

✝

DEDICATION

To our Blessed Mother Mary and to St. Padre Pio,
for teaching me to do all for the glory of God,
the Father, the Son, and the Holy Spirit.

✝

"O Blessed Rosary of Mary,
sweet chain which unites us to God,
bond of love which unites us to the angels,
tower of salvation against the assaults of Hell,
safe port in our universal shipwreck,
we will never abandon you. "
(Blessed Bartolo Longo, *Supplication to the Queen of the Holy Rosary*)

✝

ACKNOWLEDGMENTS

Frank Kelly expresses his gratitude to the following people:

To my parents, Thomas and Margaret, for handing the Catholic Faith on to me.

To my spiritual director, Father Ron Tacelli, for his initial encouragement regarding this book and for writing its Preface.

To St. Luke, portrayer of our Lady, for his intercession with the Lord inspiring us with the concept for the cover design of the book.

To David L. Vise for coming up with the book's title.

To all the people who were willing to share their kind and wonderful testimonials for this book at the request of David Lang.

To Lawrence F. Roberge, author of his own book *The Cost of Abortion*, for his help with the legal work for this book.

To Brian P. Marchionni for his advisory consultations and assistance with the logistics involved in the first two printings of this book.

To Ahrens Design for implementing the cover as we desired.

To all those who contributed in any way, through their deeds and/or prayers (known only by God), to the production of this book.

✝

"The most high God has wrought
signs and wonders toward me.
It has seemed good to me therefore to publish His signs,
because they are great;
and His wonders, because they are mighty."
(Daniel 3:99-100, *Douay-Rheims-Challoner Translation*)

✝

"The Lord has given me a learned tongue,
that I should know how to uphold by word
him that is weary.
He wakens in the morning,
in the morning he wakens my ear,
that I may hear Him as a Master.
The Lord God has opened my ear, and I do not resist."
(Isaiah 50:4-5, *Douay-Rheims-Challoner Translation*)

✝

"Your sons and your daughters shall prophesy;
your old men shall dream dreams,
and your young men shall see visions."
(Joel 2:28, *Douay-Rheims-Challoner Translation*)

✝
CONTENTS

✝
Preface

All right. I give up. I surrender. I used to try to explain away
what was going on in Frank Kelly's life, and in the lives of those he
touched. There *has* to be a perfectly natural explanation, I used to
tell myself. Frank was so ordinary. He wouldn't stand out in a
crowd—unless you happened to notice a man whose limbs were
knotted and gnarled with arthritis but whose smile seemed to
radiate inner peace and joy. He wasn't a Scripture scholar—but he
did have this knack for quoting just the right verse to the right
person at the right time. He didn't know the correct pronunciation
of many words—but he seemed to know the words people most
needed to hear, about their deepest inner struggles: things he had
no natural way of knowing. How could this be?

Ultimately, my increasingly desperate attempts at natural
explanation came to this: electricity. On December 5, 1985, Frank
was electrocuted. (You can read all the details in his spiritual saga,
narrated in the following pages.) It was this, I thought, that had
opened him up to some other level of reality and thus to the
possibility of a knowledge not accessible to the rest of us. But
what was this "other" level of reality? I was really telling myself
that a perfectly natural phenomenon like electricity had helped
Frank to reach a level of knowledge above or beyond what is
normal or natural for human beings. Which of course could only
mean that Frank was actually in touch with a more-than-natural
reality. So the harder I tried to keep the explanation perfectly and
completely natural, the more I was forced to confront the supernatural.

This should not have surprised me. If you believe in God,

then you believe that there is more to reality than what we can see, hear, taste, or feel. In fact, the very heart of reality is more than any creature can sense. The visible world points beyond itself to the invisible mystery that grounds it. And if you are a Catholic Christian, you believe that God uses the sensible things of this world—ordinary things like bread, wine, and water—to share His eternal Love with His creatures. It's called the sacramental principle.

God used electricity to heighten Frank's vision, to make the earthen vessel of his body receptive of realities to which most of us are blind and deaf. And He uses Frank, this very human man with his radiant smile and remarkable touch and words of knowledge, as a sensible sign of the eternal Love that lies at the heart of things: the Love that created us, sustains us, reaches out to us, and wants to heal us of hate and sin; the Love that will transform each of us into signs of Love in the world—but only if we let Him.

The circumstances of my meeting Frank are recounted in the pages of this book. There's no need to retell that story. But there are two incidents I'd like to recall here that helped me to abandon completely my one-time project of explaining Frank Kelly away.

The first occurred at a crowded mid-Summer prayer service. We were in a Church hall, as I remember, a kind of makeshift auditorium. The air was stifling. In the humid press of the crowd, a woman stood in line, waiting for a prayer. She was cradling an infant in her arms. The child could not have been more than a few months old; it was wailing uncontrollably. The woman, obviously embarrassed, was trying her best to comfort the child, but the child could not be comforted; again and again its piercing screams filled the crowded room. Finally she stood before Frank and me. But before praying over the woman, Frank moved his huge knobby hand to cup the infant's head. I gasped and almost struck Frank's hand away, fearing that he might inadvertently hurt the child. But as soon as Frank's hand rested on that tiny head (which was inches from my own), the child fell *immediately* into a peaceful sleep. The face, which seconds before had been painfully contorted, was resting on its mother's shoulder with a look of perfect contentment. Whatever else that was, it was no coincidence.

The second incident was far more dramatic. I was with Frank, in a small, rural, parish church, for the final session of a Seminar in the Spirit. A young man came forward asking for a prayer of healing. While Frank and I were praying over him, the fellow suddenly started to sway, as if he were about to lose consciousness. Then just as suddenly he jerked himself forward, as if to stay awake. This happened several times. Frank had by now moved back from the young man and was praying with unwonted intensity—an intensity so fierce that I feared for his health. And the young man, clearly feeling the wave of Frank's prayer washing over him, was alternately swaying with the wave and jerking himself forward so as not to be swept over by it. As I watched this extraordinary scene, I realized what the swaying and jerking really meant: healing was being offered to this young man tonight—and yet he was resisting! All at once I saw with the unmixed clarity of revelation, that we weren't *merely* a few people in a small church uttering sounds into the sultry New England evening. Another reality was there with us (within us and all around us)—a reality that had always been present, but was now breaking through from behind the screen of the ordinary. It was God Himself, offering the gift of healing, using his servant, this simple man, Frank Kelly, to invite one of His creatures into the great freedom of love. For a moment I caught the clearest glimpse I've ever had of the Real behind everyday reality—the Real to which Frank has been mysteriously opened.

The testimonies you're about to read in this book are all, in their way, variations on that one theme. Take them in, dear reader. Catch a glimpse.

Ronald K. Tacelli, S.J., Ph.D.
Boston College

[Note from the Author: The circumstances of Father Ronald Tacelli's involvement and his eventual role in Frank Kelly's spiritual journey can be read in two sections of this book: Frank Kelly's autobiography and my own personal testimonial.]

✝
The Remarkable Story of Francis B. Kelly
(In His Own Words)

Simple Beginnings

I was raised in Brookline, Massachusetts -- one of twelve children born to Thomas and Margaret Kelly. First and foremost I thank my mother and father for instructing me in the Faith and for setting an example. My parents had a great devotion to the Rosary, which seemed to be the main source of instruction in my life. They had the foresight to give us a good education.

I would like to thank the Sisters of St. Joseph for my time in grammar school, when I picked up the spirituality of a prayer life, revolving around dedication to the Mass, the Stations of the Cross, and great trust in God. I believed in God, for whom nothing was impossible -- even though my own life seemed to be all over the place. But my prayer life always seemed to be centered around Jesus, Mary, angels, and saints.

As a young child, every year in March and December I would run to the church for the novena in honor of St. Francis Xavier, about whose missionary work in various countries I learned from the great Jesuit preachers. What meant so much to me was his prayer life, his devotion to the Cross. I can still visualize him even today. Although it was only a statue, when I looked at it he seemed to come to life for me, when he held out that crucifix and leaned over the people. I thought it was just overwhelming. I felt a great peace around that -- the sense that God was always going to guide my life.

As a young child, I used to lie on the pew and look up at the

Jesuit priest who would come out and give instruction to the many
adults in the church. I thought it was a wonderful thing to see a
priest correcting parents in some way. When you're a child you're
so used to being yelled at, that it seemed a bit of a switch to see
adults being reprimanded. But I saw his great zeal for a prayer life,
the Mass, and how he preached the sacraments, in particular
confession, while explaining how merciful Jesus is in our life the
more we call upon Him. The hard part was to act on it. Those
experiences of wanting to make novenas occurred between the ages
of seven, eight, and nine.

At this point I want to thank the late Richard Cardinal
Cushing. With his dragged-out and gravelly Irish voice, it was a
thrill to listen to his Rosary every night. My mother would turn the
radio on and would gather those of us who were in the house to say
the Rosary. I enjoyed those times. I remember kneeling down on
the floor among my brothers and sisters -- you could feel the unity
of the family every time we did that. I always wanted to believe
that it would stay with us. But we know in today's times how
quickly we can lose that. But it did stay with me, and no matter
what I tried to do in life I always called upon our Blessed Mother
through the Rosary to help me in all my endeavors.

At the age of ten, I was hit by an automobile -- which was
quite traumatic for my whole family. I was hit on a major highway.
The driver had gone through a yellow and red light, dragging me
some distance on the wide bumper of his 1958 Cadillac. I broke my
collar bone. Even though I was wearing thick leather cowboy
boots, the accident took off all the skin on one foot. The only thing
they could do at the Children's Hospital in Boston was extend my
foot out a window to let the air get at it and watch it go through a
healing process by itself. Since the foot had to be kept stationary, I
was pretty much confined to the bed. I would often meditate about
what God could do to help me get out of this situation. I would
pray and ask Jesus and the Blessed Mother to help me, knowing in

my trust that at some point God was going to do the work --
especially because the doctors told my mother and father that there
was nothing they could do other than to wait and hope that the foot
would heal by itself. Eventually it did, and I really experienced the
first major result of trusting in God. My collar bone came back
stronger than it was before, and my foot turned out to be fine. In
fact, the accident caused the toes to turn down and inward, which
actually helped me athletically to maintain a firm grip on the ground
when running. God thus enabled me to continue participating in
something I enjoyed -- namely, sports.

Around the age of twelve I received Confirmation. To me
this was a great experience in my life. I truly believed that I was
called to be a soldier of Christ. I asked God all the time to give me
whatever He promised in this Sacrament. I prayed for the various
gifts that I knew about through the Church, the catechism, and the
sisters' teaching us concerning what was to come in Confirmation.
I just believed it and didn't have any problem with it. I prayed
about it and asked the Lord that I might receive whatever He
wanted me to receive. To this day I remember it and still can feel it
when Bishop Minehan hit my cheek, knowing that there was some
awakening that promised to mean something even more in my life.
Our God was instructing me to enter a deeper spiritual life.

At the age of fourteen I had another traumatic experience --
this time almost losing an eye. I was at a school yard and one of
my classmates accidentally hit me from behind, and I fell to the
ground. I had a pencil in my hand, and the pencil stuck under my
right eye. The doctors thought there was going to be damage to
my eye and face. But again I had no fear. I trusted in God that He
would straighten things out. The pencil was removed and no
damage resulted to the eye. To most people seeing it, it looked
more frightful than it was. So once again there was a trust in God.

From listening to priests I developed a devotion to various
saints, such as St. Francis Xavier, St. Ignatius Loyola, and others. I

learned to call on the saints for different things in my life. I knew that they were going to be very important in my life, although I didn't know why. I just knew I had to pray and ask for their intercession.

During my high school days I enjoyed athletics. Education was a struggle for me. At that time I had a hearing problem that was undiagnosed. So I couldn't pick up Latin, which was a disappointment for me, because when I was a child we had the Latin Mass. But I never felt any bitterness toward God; I simply couldn't learn the Latin. At that time I didn't understand why, because my brothers Tom, John, and Joe were altar boys. I longed to follow in their footsteps by being an altar boy too. Monsignor Joseph Robinson took care to make sure that the altar boys knew all the Mass prayers, such as the Confiteor and the Creed, in Latin. But I was embarrassed that I couldn't fake it, so I had to give up the idea of being an altar boy. It disturbed me, but it didn't affect my belief or trust in God. I just felt that I had to apply myself to something else.

During this period I was having trouble in my schoolwork. I found out through this difficulty that I had to pray a lot to get answers to some things, because I was hearing improperly certain lessons. Those subjects that were taught on the blackboard, such as mathematics and science, I had no problem with. But with subjects that had to be spoken, such as English, French, Latin, and history, I was not hearing the words properly, although I didn't realize that at the time. It was not until my senior year in high school that I found out about my hearing abnormality. It happened in a classroom where the teacher had a very loud voice. He told us to turn to page number twenty-two. To me it just sounded like "oo-oo". Since I didn't quite hear what the numbers were, I turned around and asked the gentleman behind me what page the teacher said. The teacher happened to hear me ask this question, and had me sent to the school clinic to have my ears examined (after a humorous remark about it). When I got there, the nurse realized that the teacher who referred me had a very loud voice. Therefore, she did more extensive testing in which the volume was turned up, and it was finally discovered that I wasn't hearing words properly.

So I was then sent to Massachusetts Eye and Ear Hospital in Boston to have my ears examined. In this process their doctor was quite surprised to discover that I didn't have a speech impediment, since I had inner ear trouble. He wondered how I could have even gotten through school up to my senior year in high school. It was a blessing athletically that loud noises didn't disturb me, such as the sounds of the crowd in the stands, although it hadn't been such a blessing for my schoolwork. I also thought, once again, that Jesus and the Blessed Mother were helping me.

I later went to a small business college, majored in accounting, and got an associate's degree. I played basketball. My life wasn't anything special. Whenever I could I would attend Mass. I was always faithful to Mass on Sundays, holydays, and certain other times of the year, and went to confession at least once a year. That was the permanent foundation, but I would try to go a little bit beyond the basic rules of the Church, such as by going to confession as frequently as I could. I always stayed close to my Rosary, no matter what was going on in my life. That was part of me all the time.

Marriage and Family

Eventually, after I graduated, I met my wife-to-be Joanne. It was funny: people had often told me that if I were ever going to get married I'd have to meet someone in a gymnasium or a baseball field. That's what my mother always used to say, because I was involved in sports so much. So there was a bit of a prophetic message there, because I did meet my future wife in a gymnasium.

During courtship, as at all other times, I always wanted to

follow everything the Church teaches. It was very important to me to be obedient to God, because it seemed that anytime I didn't abide by that my whole life was disturbed. When I was with God, I was at peace -- no matter what was happening outside me. God promised me that peace, and I believe I received it. I believe that peace came from the day when the bishop hit my cheek at Confirmation. I always believed that if I remained obedient to God and the Church, then my peace would stay; outside that way, I would lose my peace.

Eventually, Joanne and I did marry. We married in 1970. We had our daughter Debra in 1972 and our son Joseph in 1975. Again in our marital life, whenever I could get to daily Mass I would go, and I would say the Rosary during whatever spare time I had -- in particular on the way traveling to and from work. Retrospectively, I wish we had prayed more as a family. I feel that I didn't do all I could have done for us by way of instruction in this area. I kept my prayer life separate to myself and didn't share it with my family as much as I should have -- which I regret today. But that doesn't mean I didn't share it at all, because my son has picked it up, and I do believe he has been touched very much.

Before Joseph's birth, when I was working insulating pipes at a paper-mill in Jay, Maine, I fell out of a section of gang pipe. I fell forty feet and was heading for something that looked to me like a cardboard shield protecting the big paper machine. I thought I was going to crash through it and become pulp in the machine. As I came down, I heard a voice within me telling me to turn. When I hit the shield (with my body turned on my hip), I found out that is was actually plexiglass from which I bounced up as on a trampoline. I flattened out and grabbed the ribs and the top of the plexiglass with my two hands. I just lay there and the voice within me told me not to move. Eventually they came up and got me off the shield and down onto the catwalk. They were surprised I was fine: I broke no bones and had no injuries. They told me the normal reaction would have been to let go. But that would have caused me to slide into the machine, so it was a good thing I didn't move. They were more shaken up than I was. Later I realized that it had been my guardian angel speaking to me for my protection.

During our marriage a very sad episode occurred. Our son Joseph came down with spinal meningitis. They told us it could be fatal, and gave him only twenty-seven hours. If he did recover, he would most likely suffer damaging after-effects that would remain for the rest of his life. It was very scary to be told that. We had just taken him to the hospital the day before (on Sunday), when the doctor told my wife that it looked like our son had measles -- a misdiagnosis, as it turned out. I remember I was working out of state (in Maine) and had to leave that night to prepare for work on Monday. But I had to come all the way back from Maine after being there only a couple of hours. I was called back after my wife drove Joseph to the hospital again very early Monday morning, when his condition worsened. This time they correctly diagnosed the meningitis. When I returned and saw my wife, the expression on her face was not hopeful. She said that things didn't look good, that it looked like he was not going to make it. When I went into the room where my son was, I saw nothing but doctors. I looked in and asked the doctors if I could at least see him. One doctor asked me who I was. When I replied that I was his father, I was told that the pupils of his eyes had just moved, so I should lean over his bed and start talking. And that's what I did. I talked and prayed, and prayed and talked, until I couldn't talk or pray anymore with my tired vocal cords. The doctor said that they didn't know what would happen now. So I left the room, went out to my wife, and told her not to worry, but just to pray to Padre Pio for his intercession. I told her that I was going to pray.

I then went to Mission Church in the Roxbury section of Boston, where many miracles had occurred before the large picture of Our Lady of Perpetual Help. (Many times my own mother and father had taken us there to be blessed by a priest holding a small picture after the end of the weekly novena to Our Lady of Perpetual Help.) I looked up and asked the Mother of God to intercede to bring my son back healthy. Between tears and prayers, I came home knowing and believing in my heart that he would be fine. In the next ten to twelve days, the medicine worked, and Joseph kept getting stronger. Doctors today would probably call it somewhat of a miracle.

There is an interesting connection here. There have been saints and servants of God who have been sources of miraculous signs for people in my life. One of them is Padre Pio, who was invoked for a successful cure of spinal meningitis for someone in Italy -- which was the cure used for his canonization (as I later found out). Another one is Fr. Nelson Baker, a Servant of God from Buffalo, New York, to whom I pray for his intercession. He also intervened for someone with spinal meningitis. Both were truly instances of miraculous cures. This recalls to my mind when my son had spinal meningitis. I knew that through the intercession of Padre Pio, along with the Blessed Mother, everything would be fine if I just kept praying.

At this same time my wife and I were having a new home built. Unfortunately that house was not constructed properly on solid ground with the right supports. After a while the floors actually sank and the foundation cracked, so the walls also cracked at stress points. The builder kept refusing to repair it -- which put a lot of pressure on us. (I still pray for this gentleman and his own wife and children). One day he came to my wife and threatened her, telling her that her husband was trying to trap him and that there would be a long drawn-out fight over this. But I kept telling Joanne not to worry: all we had to do was fix just what had to be fixed. Eventually things got done and we settled out of court, as Scripture advises.

But it was too much pressure for my wife and me to bear

along with the stress of Joseph's illness. I thought there may also have been stress over my inability to hear properly. Around this time (the end of 1983) when I was an insulating foreman, since I still couldn't hear properly, I went back to get my ears re-examined. They recommended hearing aids for the inner ear problems I had in both ears, because I could hear sounds but couldn't make out distinct words. I had only fifty percent hearing, which they thought was caused by the fact that at birth the umbilical cord was wrapped around my head. At this time I thought it was a healing for my hearing trouble, because I started to hear words I had never heard properly (for example, the difference between "stop" and "shop") and sounds I had never heard at all before (such as the car directional blinkers and the click of a light-switch). I also realized my voice was louder than I thought, which could have contributed to the marital strain. Believing as St. Paul says in the Scriptures, we separated and I prayed for her.

Then a friend (Richard Colfer, a pharmacist) called me up and told me that his wife had left him and had taken their children, moving to New York. He asked me to come and live with him rent-free. While living with Rich, I started going to daily Mass and saying daily Rosary, asking the Lord: "If my heart was not right, please change it." This lasted for almost two years.

Shocking Events

During this period after my separation from Joanne, I was electrocuted -- on December 5, 1985. I was lying in some crawl-space on top of a walk-in refrigerator in order to reach some pipes, when my right wrist came in contact with four lines of exposed electrical wiring that protruded through a junction box. (These wires ran through the whole hospital at the construction project site where I was working as a foreman.) The electricity went through my hips, and then came out through my hips, my calves, and my feet. I was basically left to die, because they didn't think anyone could survive the current that went through my whole body. How they got me out of the crawl-space is the first thing I never understood, but eventually I did wake up afterwards in the hospital. Right away I sat up, but some doctor or internist there tried to push me back down, because (as I was told) a dead body sometimes pops up. Every joint felt like it was burning. I said that I had to go the bathroom and tried to get up, but felt wobbly. So I lay back down, realizing I lacked the strength to get up. The doctor on duty headed out the door (evidently in shock). I think he had a clip-board in his hands. As I found out later, he was apparently waiting for me to die with a death-certificate on the clip-board, because no one had ever survived this type of electrocution. He returned with the doctors in charge. Many other doctors came in after that and looked at me, asking questions about how I felt and whether I knew what had happened. (I remembered very little.) They monitored my heart for twenty-nine days, because every six days my heart would stop for eleven seconds and then come back on the twelfth second. The head cardiologist, Dr. Mark Estes, diagnosed the need for a pacemaker, because they didn't want to send me home with my erratic heartbeat.

But I had tremendous fear of operations; I would pass out even at the sight of a needle. I was praying in a state of fear, when suddenly Padre Pio himself walked into the hospital room and told me everything would be alright. Then a tremendous peace came over me and I had no more fear of the operation -- the fear left me immediately and I was ready for the surgery. While I was under general anesthesia (apparently unconscious), I "heard" the main surgeon tell his assistant to stitch me up because he had to catch a flight to Miami. When the main surgeon came back to see me in my room a few days later, I asked him how his trip to Miami went. He was shocked because he knew I was under total anesthesia. It was at this point that I realized something was happening to me.

From that point on I had nothing but a fervent prayer life.

I came home to recuperate at Rich's house. They told me it would take four to six weeks to recover. I asked them if I could then go back to work and they said, yes, after six weeks. The following day I went to daily Mass at my parish church (St. Mary's in Foxboro). I asked Padre Pio, if there was more to this, then he was going to have to help me. So I was kneeling down after Mass saying my Rosary and was asking for the intercession of Padre Pio. Suddenly a certain woman (Marion, who later became my prayer partner) came down the church aisle abruptly to me. To me she looked as though she was flying down the aisle like an angel. She tapped me on the shoulder, and told me that I should go to Fr. Babbitt's parish (St. Mary's in North Attleboro) on Thursday night.

Later that same day I drove to the local Shrine of Our Lady of LaSalette (in Attleboro) and found it to be a home, knowing that I would be back there daily. (I had never been there before.) On Thursday evening I went to Fr. Babbitt's. I went to confession, when he did pray over me -- the first time this had ever happened to me. I then attended his Mass. In his homiletic message he mentioned a healing that he personally had received through the intercession of Padre Pio. At the end of Mass I started to leave, but Marion tried to stop me, asking me whether I would stay to get prayed over. At that time I didn't know what she was talking about, because I didn't know anything about people being prayed over. So I left.

I woke up the next day (Friday) and went to Mass. I saw Marion there and asked her whether there was a prayer group around, which I pictured to myself would be a Padre Pio prayer group. She responded that there was a neighboring parish (St. Mary's in Wrentham) that had a small prayer meeting every Monday night. We drove there together the following Monday night, and walked into the little chapel where the group met. The woman (Phyllis) we encountered inside the chapel whispered out to please turn on the light. I snapped the light-switch on, and saw at the light-switch a novena prayer to Padre Pio! Needless to say, I felt very much at home. We sat down, said some prayers along with the Rosary (which gave me a sense of peace) and the Divine Mercy chaplet. Then the people there started to do some "witnessing" (which I didn't know about at the time). It was funny that the gentleman to my left (whose name I later learned was Dan) looked just like Padre Pio, complete with a beard; it was as though I was seeing things.

When they got around to asking me why I came there, I replied that I had prayed to God and asked for the intercession of Padre Pio -- I knew that Padre Pio had prayer groups. I told them the whole story of how Padre Pio had led me to their prayer group, including Marion urging me to come there and then seeing the Padre Pio novena prayer at the light-switch. I wound up telling them about my life -- about the electrocution and how Padre Pio had appeared to me in my hospital room and so on.

But then I was taken aback when a gentleman there (a Roman Catholic) looked at me and said that the saints wouldn't have brought you here -- only Jesus could bring you here. Then Dan spoke up in my defense, saying that I had described Padre Pio to the letter, because he had attended Padre Pio's actual Mass a number of times when he was in the service stationed in Italy during World War II. Then I brought up that the saints will instruct you and lead you to Jesus. The saints can lead you to God and to Mary, just as Mary will lead you to Jesus. After this setback, I didn't know whether I wanted to stay with this group.

But I went home and prayed, and decided to go back the next week. Phyllis told me that I had given quite a witnessing the previous week. She suggested that maybe the Lord wanted to use me in a strong way. I replied that I didn't know. She asked me whether I had ever made a "Life-in-the-Spirit" seminar. I told her no, that I didn't even know what it was. She said that they were going to be holding one at another local parish. So she led us over to that parish (St. Mary's in Franklin), where I was given a book that I was very happy with, about making a Life-in-the-Spirit seminar. It covered sacraments, saints, everything that our Church teaches. I really took to heart the daily meditations in the book, each day asking God to show me how that meditation applied to me that day.

In this process my prayer life had become fervent. Eventually, with the grace of God, I was able to start walking again. I would go to the Shrine of Our Lady of LaSalette, known also as the Lady of Reconciliation. That contributed more to my prayer life, and I was now walking constantly while praying. I would say four sets of the five-decade Rosary kneeling, four sets walking, and four sets sitting -- a total of sixty five-decade Rosaries. Also I would make the Stations of the Cross and attend Mass. At the shrine I would spend about an hour-and-a-half in prayer, asking the Lord how He wanted me to pray. I would find prayer cards that I kept for the intercession of various saints for different people.

God was doing something in my life. But the greatest thrill was my guardian angel leading me to Eucharistic adoration. I spent as much time as I could in adoration of the Blessed Sacrament, eventually finding a church (St. Mary's in Taunton) that held adoration from 8 o'clock in the morning to 8 o'clock at night. In the meantime, I would be awakened and guided to churches that had adoration when I didn't even know the location of such churches in advance! So these things were happening in my life. I didn't really know what I was doing, but I kept being led to adoration of God. Beyond my prayers at LaSalette shrine, the rest of my time every day I would spend two to five hours sitting in adoration before the Blessed Sacrament.

But even after the pacemaker was implanted and I now had the ability to walk, the pain I had still didn't seem to subside. I remember, when I got home to Rich's house, asking the Lord to correct whatever was wrong with my heart. What He had really done was to give me a new heart. I had more zeal for God. I just started praying more and couldn't stop praying. I kept saying to God: You show me how to pray, You teach me how to pray. It seems that I would be getting saints' prayers: numerous saints from St. Benedict to St. Dominic to St. Francis Xavier. All these saints would come into my head to pray to for their intercession.

I had much difficulty getting out of bed and moving about on account of the pain I had. I kept going back and complaining to the doctors about it, but they kept telling me I was fit to return to work. But I found I could no longer play basketball. Then finally the pain got so bad that I actually had to fall out of bed just to get up, pushing my back against the bed for support. The doctors didn't know at first what was wrong with me, but eventually diagnosed me with rheumatoid arthritis that had set in. One doctor said he believed this resulted from the shock to the body in the electrocution. But that's something for the medical people to debate.

So then I realized I was completely in the hands of God. I had no idea what I was going to do financially, since I was no longer able to work at a paying job. I told God: I'm totally yours now. In the two-year period after the Life-in-the-Spirit seminar all I did was continue to pray unceasingly, as St. Paul would say.

Family Rupture

Little by little as these things were happening, things were moving much faster between my wife and me. Joanne decided to pursue a divorce. This put a strain on the family, because Debra chose to live with her mother and Joseph chose to live with his father. So at this point I had to get an apartment. But I basically had no money, at this time being on workman's compensation. I needed money for the first and last month's rent, which I didn't have; if anything, I had just enough money to pay one month's rent. In fact, prior to the divorce, I gave my wife the weekly check without questioning anything. It was only after she made her decision that she wanted the divorce that I took the money. I had to do what the court was telling us to do. Then the situation was in man' hands, and it became a real mess. But I never had any animosity against my wife, and I pray daily for her. Whatever God wanted, His will would be done -- not mine. I never looked to the Church for any way out. I don't feel that an annulment is the proper thing to seek, if the sacrament of Matrimony was received in the Church. From that day to the present, in the eyes of God I am married and will always be married. I defend the sacrament of Marriage, because I respect the sacraments and I believe that once married, always married. I still love my wife, I love my daughter, and I love my son -- as I love God. God will always be first and I will always seek God to help me. My trust and my faith is in God to heal whatever has to be healed in my family. I will never stop praying for my family, as well as for other people.

As I mentioned earlier, my friend Rich was a great gift from God with his tremendous help. But eventually I had to apply for an apartment. As I said, I didn't know whether I needed the money for both the first and last month's rent, because I had enough money only for one month's rent. But when I went to look at a certain duplex apartment, the landlord said all he wanted was one month's rent. He even said not to pay him until the end of the month -- which I felt was truly a gift from God.

This apartment was in the same town as the house where my wife and I had been living -- I was just moving to a different section of the town. So I went home to bring my son back with me in the car to see the apartment. As we were driving, Joe remarked to me that it seemed far away from his friends. I told him that I wasn't putting any pressure on him. If he wanted, he could stay with his mom, but at least he would know where I was -- I would show him. When we arrived at the apartment, he went in and looked around. Then he came back out and exclaimed: "Dad, great place! We're going to get it!" But I answered that it had not been officially given to me yet. He said, "Oh, no. We're going to get it, Dad, because the man's son is my best friend at school." So it seemed to me it was a good thing that God had me bring my son with me. We did get the apartment and moved in.

Unusual Occurrences

Thereafter, it seems that God just kept working. My prayer life was out of control in the sense that I didn't have a spiritual director. I knew I had to get one, but just wasn't sure what I should get a spiritual director *for* at the time.

At this point I want to begin relating some special encounters in my life. I want to emphasize that I'm no better than anyone else. I just prayed daily that God would instruct me.

When I used to walk around LaSalette Shrine, I would hear a voice inside me. I didn't know what to say about it to anybody, other than that I kept constantly hearing: "Go instruct, go instruct." I used to answer: "Instruct *what*?". And I would just keep walking.

Now at that time I smoked cigarettes -- not that much, but enough so that it obviously disturbed the Lord (as I would later find out). In my stay with Rich, I learned more and more about angels. When I was working before my injury, I prayed whenever I could. And on two different occasions I "saw" what I can only describe as "neon signs" in front of me: white lights surrounding big bluish-purplish letters that told me "STOP SMOKING". I ignored them; I would brush them away with my hands. One person even looked at me and asked me whether there was something wrong with me, because I was coming out of a room as though there was something in front of the door. I didn't want to reply that I was just pushing some letters away. But later on I realized that, since an angel can take on various forms, it was my own guardian angel communicating with me this way to tell me to stop smoking. All this happened during my stay with Rich.

Well, when night came on the particular day when we moved in to our new apartment (with all kinds of cartons and boxes around), I sent Joey upstairs to his room and prayed to God that he would sleep well, that he would feel comfortable and at peace with his decision to stay with me (he was only in the sixth grade). I thought to myself that this was going to be quite a struggle. But then I thought, no, we got in here, so nothing will happen. I was sitting on the couch smoking a cigarette, feeling relieved that we were all moved in to our own place now, while at the same time saying to God that I believed it was going to take a lot of prayer to help this family to heal what should be healed. (I think psychological problems are harder to overcome than physical ones.) Anyway, after I finished smoking this cigarette, I reached down for another one and realized I had none left. I decided to get in the car and drive to an all-night gas station to pick up another pack of cigarettes. I drove back home, went into the apartment, sat down, and decided to light up one more cigarette before I went to bed. Sitting at the end of my couch, I had just lit up the cigarette when I looked over -- and there was Jesus, sitting there looking at me from the other end of the couch. He told me to put the cigarette out, and then said: "I even tried to save you money." (I then recalled about the neon signs stating: "STOP SMOKING".) He looked at me and said: "From now on you will never smoke again." He stood up, walked over to me, took me by my right hand and said: "Come with me." He walked me out to the kitchen. Then He told me to place my cigarettes on top of the refrigerator. After I placed the pack on top of the refrigerator, He guided me back out to the living room. He stood by the door and said: "This is an answer to your son's prayer." That nearly knocked me to the floor -- knowing that my son had been praying I would stop smoking. He then said to me: "When your son wakes up tomorrow, tell him do what he wants to do." Finally He said: "From now on, *I* take over." And He left, walking right through the solid closed door.

I was not dreaming. I was fully awake, wide awake, knowing what had happened. I went up to my bed, prayed and thanked Him for coming to me as the Good Shepherd (dressed in white and red robes). I had no fear and total peace. But I pondered what He said: "From now on I take over". I asked myself: "take over *what*?" Then I fell asleep.

The next morning when Joey got up, I said to him: "Do what you want to do." Immediately he went directly to the refrigerator, reached up to the top, took down the pack of cigarettes, and without saying a word destroyed them all -- crushing them and ripping them up. Now bear in mind there was no way he could have known that I had put a pack of cigarettes up there. You would think he would have gone to my shirt pocket, because that's where I always kept them. He threw the cigarettes in the trashbag, and I ended up taking them myself to the dumpster. (And to think I could have saved money, because there were still nineteen cigarettes left in the pack!) I have never smoked a cigarette since that time -- not even an urge nor any withdrawal symptoms. I realized that Jesus never smoked, so He wanted me to imitate Him as much as possible.

This episode left me with a tremendous longing to pray unceasingly, as St. Paul advises. I started to understand Scripture, like I could never understand Scripture before. People would read verses and say it meant one thing, when it would have an altogether different meaning to me. Quite often it would scare me, although my spiritual director today would call it theologically sound. For the first time in my life, I experienced what Jesus said to the Apostles: "I will send you the Paraclete, who will remind you of everything." St. Francis Xavier said that everyone learns one line from Scripture that stays with them. The line from Scripture that I heard as a child and that stayed with me was: "I am going to leave you many signs and wonders." So, with Jesus showing up and saying "From now on I take over", I knew I had to continue to seek Him and He would tell me what I was to instruct.

A few days after the encounter with Jesus, I was walking around LaSalette praying again as usual, but then I started asking God questions. One of the questions I asked was: "Why did I used to make the novenas to St. Francis Xavier every March and December at my parish church?" I went down to the shrine bookstore and opened an ordinary book, and the line I saw read like this: "When St. Francis Xavier entered India, he could not reach the adults. In praying the Lord inspired him to speak to the children, and the children would bring the adults." When I closed the book, I went to continue walking around praying, and the voice said to me: "You were the child at the novena." So then I understood that God was already calling me for something at an early age when the Jesuit priest would give the twice-yearly novena. It shocked me to hear the voice say that I was the child at the novena. I continued to meditate on that the rest of the day.

Shortly after that, I was doing my daily prayers in my room kneeling down. Suddenly I had a vision. The room was totally illuminated as with a heavenly light -- lit up very brightly, more than a big cinema screen. It was overwhelming, but had my full attention. In front of me was a priest walking toward a kneeler. He was dressed the way I used to see priests enter the confessional -- wearing a black cassock with white lace, a purple stole, and a biretta on his head. He was facing the congregation, but I was the only person in the church. It was the parish church of my childhood. I was feeling the same way I felt when I used to go to the novenas in honor of St. Francis Xavier -- a sense of trust in God. The priest knelt down on the kneeler, reached underneath to the book-holder, and pulled out a fish. He looked at me and threw the fish at me. When I tried to grab the fish, it bounced out of my hand and slid halfway down the bench toward him. He retrieved the fish and then threw it at me a second time. I caught the fish, and the vision ended. Both the heavenly light and the whole scene were extinguished.

I knew I had to pray to understand the meaning of this vision in light of what Jesus said when He left me: "From now on I take over." I knew in my heart from Scripture to read Daniel, who is the patron saint of all visions. Of course, to test whether a vision comes from God, one should command: "In the name of Jesus Christ, go away." If it doesn't go away, it comes from God. I learned that from Padre Pio. In fact, I had done just that during the first part of the vision when the priest started walking toward the kneeler, but the vision continued anyway. So I knew this *was* of God.

I knew from Daniel that visions are for yourself before you get a correct interpretation. So when the vision ended, it left me with a longing to keep praying that God would teach me what He wanted me to understand. I went to several prayer groups and asked different people for their interpretation. I would get responses such as "God wants you to catch men." But it wasn't the answer, because St. Peter was a priest but I was a layman. I also went to a priest and told him about the vision, and he asked whether it was him in the vision. I walked away disappointed, because it wasn't him. So I kept praying: "Lord, please, guide me to the person who will give me the answer." I never prayed for my own little personal healings, other than that the Sacraments would bear fruit in my life the way God wanted them to be fulfilled -- not the way I wanted them to be fulfilled.

I had read as much as I could about Padre Pio who had many, fairly rare gifts. I had always been taught that such gifts were apostolic. (I don't care to use the word "charismatic"; I prefer the word "apostolic".) I wanted to be apostolic, because the instruction in my head all the time about the Church was "one, holy, catholic, and apostolic". I wanted to stay faithful to the teaching of the Church's Magisterium. So I asked Padre Pio to help me.

Eventually a friend of mine by the name of Rheta, who knew I was still looking for an answer to the vision, led me to a healing service in Worcester, conducted by a woman whose name is Eileen George. She was a grandmother who had cancer of the lymph nodes, at one point being told that she had only two weeks to live. Now Rheta told me ahead of time that sometimes when Mrs. George moves around the church, you can smell the scent of roses. I didn't go to smell roses, because that didn't strike me. But the smell of roses meant to me another calling from Padre Pio to go. I always felt that Pio, along with my guardian angel, was at my side to lead me to the right people. So Mrs. George came out and began talking about "Daddy God" (that's just how she said it). Well, my entire body was filled with joy, because that was the first time I had ever heard someone speak of "Daddy God" the way I called *my* Father God "Daddy God". I felt so free with the abundance of God's love in me that I wanted to give it away -- I could have embraced everybody in the church. When Eileen continued the healing service and had a word of knowledge about a healing, she would just point to the person and state the healing. As she walked down the aisle, I smelled the tremendous fragrance of roses. After the service I went to the back of the church to pick up all the itinerary schedules and news reports of Eileen George.

Charismatic Gifts

The next day (Monday) I was walking at LaSalette as usual and came upon a gentleman by the name of Joe, whom on many occasions I saw at different prayer groups. Every time the people in the groups would pray in tongues, when he gave the interpretation I knew it was on the money. So when I met him that day, knowing his charism of interpretation of tongues, I shared about Eileen George and give him her itinerary that I had taken from the church. The inner voice said to me: "Tell him about the vision." So I explained to him the whole vision. He went into the chapel to pray, while I was still outside walking and praying. Shortly thereafter Joe came out and approached me. He said to me: "In the vision you never saw the face on the priest." I then realized that he knew, because I thought I had to find the priest in this vision. He next said to me: "The reason you didn't see a face on the priest was because your messages come directly from the Father and no one has ever seen the Father." As soon as Joe said that I felt totally free, knowing that this was the correct interpretation of the vision. Then he added: "The reason you get the messages from the Father is that He wants to use you to heal man." But *that* I rejected and walked away. (At that time I never thought about the meaning of the fish, but now I realize the connection with what Jesus said to St. Peter about catching men. This also goes back to the interpretation of the words of the voice saying "Go instruct", because God used Peter to instruct and convert, and God wanted to use me to instruct for conversion and healing.)

I went up to the Calvary crucifix by way of the holy stairs, thanking God for the interpretation, but telling the Lord that I was not worthy of the healing part. I came down the stairs and was leaving, heading for my car, when Joe approached me again. He said to me: "Are you wondering how the Lord is going to use you to heal people?" I said no, and I wasn't concerned. He said: "You just have to speak and the Lord will heal." Again I rejected that and continued to my car, when the inner voice gave me my first Scriptural reading (Acts 3:1-10). When I got home I read it, and this confirmed what Joe had said: all I had to do was speak.

The next day Joe called me and we had a conversation on the phone. During this conversation he thanked me for answering a problem just by speaking with him. This went on for a couple of weeks.

In the meantime, whenever I said the Our Father in the Rosary, I was having difficulty saying the word "trespasses". One day later, as I was going to Eucharistic adoration with Marion, we started saying the Rosary in the car. When I came to this particular word in the Our Father, an "utterance" came over me. I found myself uttering sounds loudly. Marion said that it was "angelical prayer" (or "tongues"), and it was about time that I did it. I hadn't allowed myself to let go before this point. Now I couldn't stop. It became overwhelming. I just kept doing it until we arrived at the church. I realized at adoration that I could control it and use it whenever I needed it (whether silently or aloud).

On my next trip to see Eileen George, both my friends Joe and Carmelita came along with me to the service. On our way there I discussed with them how they should pray more to their guardian angels and also invoke the other choirs of angels. After Eileen's teaching, there was a break. Joe went downstairs and picked up a book on guardian angels, handed it to me, and asked me to look at it. Then the healing part of the service started. When Eileen finished her prayer, she started walking down the aisle. Approximately seven pews away from me, she announced that the Lord was healing someone's ears and she pointed directly at me, saying it was me. My two ears became inflamed. In fact, both Joe and Carmelita commented on how red they were. They were so warm that I had to remove the hearing aids. I've never had to put them back in again. My hearing is now normal. But since I never went to speech therapy, I must sometimes listen carefully to certain words that I would be hearing correctly for the first time.

About a month later, Joe called me and suggested that I go and see Fr. Robert DeGrandis. He took me to St. Anne's in Fall River for a workshop with Fr. DeGrandis. When we walked in, Fr. DeGrandis asked everyone who could pray in tongues to do so. He separated all those who could from the rest of the people. The people who could not pray in tongues he sent to a workshop there for praying in tongues. The rest of the group he divided into two parts. He asked how many wanted to learn about prophecy, and these he sent to a workshop there on prophecy. He told the rest of the people to follow him to a healing class.

Joe insisted that we follow Father wherever he was going and learn about whatever he was instructing. So we wound up in the healing workshop. We were in a third-grade classroom sitting at cramped desks. As Father started to ask questions, he asked people to raise their hands. The first question he asked was whether anyone ever got an answer from God from a regular book (other than the Bible). I raised my hand. Since I was the only one to raise his hand, I felt out of place and wanted to leave. He asked four more questions, all of which led me to raise my hand. Then he asked the last five questions, all pertaining to charismatic gifts. To these questions, everyone but me raised their hands. When he finished, he approached me and said: "Let's start praying in tongues." We started to pray in tongues together, but as soon as he said "Amen" we both stopped. Then he said to me: "You are a good Roman Catholic who is constipated and who we have to get the gifts out of." Then he looked at me and told me to put my hand on the shoulder of the woman sitting at the desk next to me. I didn't want to do that, telling Father that I would go to a mountain to pray for this woman but would not put my hand on her shoulder. When I looked back at him, his collar enlarged to four times its normal size. I now knew that I must obey him. I then put my hand on her shoulder and prayed angelically. He walked away and finally yelled "Amen" again, and I stopped. Then he said: "Would you please tell her what you saw?" I was quite surprised that he knew I saw something. He said to me: "What was it that you saw?" I said: "Boat". He walked over to me, and then he said: "Did you see a boat?" I said: "No." But then he asked how I knew it was a boat.

I said: "I saw the letters B-O-A-T." He asked me the colors. I told him they were outlined in white, blue, and purple. He replied: "That means it's a healing of a boat." The woman was startled. Then she looked at me and said: "I've never seen you before." I told her the same thing. But then she said that she had been praying for five years that her husband would not buy this boat for which he had been saving. I told her that he would not buy the boat. Again I wanted to leave the classroom immediately. But because of the rheumatoid arthritis I had swollen up and could not get out of the desk.

They then had a coffee break. Joe went to buy me coffee because I could not free myself from the desk. The woman next to me also stayed reading her notes. A man came into the classroom and sat down on the floor between our two desks. He looked at the woman and said: "Honey, you know that boat I wanted to buy? I've lost all interest in purchasing it." The woman was startled again, and told her husband (who had been in the prophecy workshop) what had happened. He was stunned, too. Then everyone came back to the classroom to continue the session. She announced to Father what had happened during the coffee break. Father came over to me and said: "Continue to use this gift: it is of God."

As they continued the class, people started asking questions about healing. There was a gentleman there that I knew who would call out healings at a healing service. He would describe the bones and where the pain was, because he claimed he would experience the same pain. He would say that the Lord was healing that particular ailment. I always felt uncomfortable about this, that there was something wrong here. When he told Father in detail what was happening to him, Father eased my concern by saying to him that this was not of God, that God would not give him someone else's pain. I thought it sounded suspicious, because I couldn't figure out how he could be standing with all this pain. So Father confirmed my suspicion, and told the man to stop. He was actually a charlatan who knew about bones from working with a nurse.

Father also told me that from now on when I see something like a picture or a word, I should ask God to explain it in detail. Driving home with Joe, I was contemplating whether I should use this gift.

Using the Word of Knowledge

The next day I went to the noon Mass at LaSalette Shrine. I was sitting in the back row of the chapel, when the Lord gave me a word of knowledge about the woman sitting next to me. I understood that she was praying for her two brothers. The Lord told me to tell this to her. I replied to Him: "You tell her." I said nothing to the woman, and left the chapel after Mass. On my way downstairs to the shrine coffee shop, I said to myself that she was probably not charismatic so she wouldn't understand -- I was rationalizing it away. When I decided to leave the shrine and headed for my car, she left the chapel heading for *her* car. There were only two cars in the parking lot and they were parked next to each other: namely, mine and hers. The Lord repeated the message to tell her that she is praying for her two brothers. I still ignored it, got in my car, and drove home. That night I prayed for her two brothers and went to sleep.

The next day I went to the shrine again. On this occasion the chapel was full. There was only one empty seat in the whole place -- it was in the back row. I sat there before the noon Mass, saying my prayers. The woman to my right got up from her seat and left. I was still praying with my eyes closed, when someone else came in and sat beside me. Then the voice said again that she is praying for her two brothers. I opened my eyes and saw it was the same lady as the day before! After Mass I again heard the voice telling me to tell her that she is praying for her brothers.

Then I remembered what Fr. DeGrandis had said: I should ask the Lord to explain about the brothers. God said: "They are with me." I thought to myself: "They are dead." But God said again: "They are with me." I finally turned to the woman and said: "I understand you're praying for your two brothers." She denied it. I stood up and went to leave. The woman then grabbed me by the arm and said: "I'm sorry. I was praying for my two brothers-in-law who just died." Then I said: "They are with God in heaven." She knew what I was talking about, and I could see that she felt at peace. She asked me more questions about how I knew, but I could only tell her what I knew the Lord told me.

In the evening I still felt uneasy about this incident. The next day I returned to the shrine. I was sitting and praying in the back of the chapel after the noon Mass. The very same lady attended the Mass and was sitting in the front of the chapel after Mass. The Lord told me to tell her that a certain individual (a woman whose name I received but have forgotten) was going to knock on her door the next morning at nine o'clock, so she should stay home to meet this person who needed her assistance. She asked me how I knew the name of this acquaintance of hers. I replied that I didn't know her, but that God knows her.

The next day I went to the noon Mass, and the very same lady came in -- this time with her daughter. She walked over to me and said that the woman did show up at exactly 9 AM, and that she had assisted her with what she needed. She then said that she called her daughter after this incident, and asked her to come to the noon Mass to meet the gentleman who has been giving her all this information. Her daughter's name was Barbara, whom I happened to see occasionally at a certain prayer group. Although I hadn't known her name before this, she did know my name. She thought it was all remarkable, but felt at ease because she had seen me at the prayer group. They left and went to the coffee shop. I started to pray for Barbara's mother, and said to the Lord: "Why don't you talk directly to her?" God said: "Frank, she has the gift of angelical prayer, but doesn't use it." Then I said: "Well, I'll fix that."

So I left the chapel and went to the coffee shop. The two were sitting there when I approached the mother and said to her in a commanding voice: "You pray angelically." She replied: "No, I don't." I said: "God doesn't lie." Then she said that once she made a Life-in-the-Spirit seminar with a prayer group and was prayed over for the renewal of the Holy Spirit in her life, went home, and was praying in this odd sound. Her husband told her to stop it and not to do it again. I told her to go to her upper room and do it there, but not in front of him, and the Lord would speak to her about whatever she needs. I left, thinking I wouldn't be bothered by God over this anymore.

From that point on I would just continue to walk around LaSalette praying, but would sometimes have conversations with various people. If the Lord told me to say something, I did say it -- but as though I had no control over it.

I still went to the prayer group at St. Mary's church in Franklin, but found at times that I had to correct some things that were said there. Whenever I said something in correction, I noticed that David never objected. So I felt at peace, and the Lord told me to pray with him. Rheta mentioned that I should start praying over people. I didn't take her advice right away. In praying, I was told by the Lord only to pray over David that night. I did not know David until Rheta told me he was studying philosophy. I did not have to say anything to David, because he came and sat beside me and asked me to pray over him -- which I did. He seemed to accept the word of knowledge, and left.

The following week Kenny came and asked for prayer. I gave him a word of knowledge. He was surprised that I knew about the matter, and went home with the advice. David then sat down and I prayed over him, telling him that I had some material for his sister. He looked at me and asked with bewilderment:

"*Which* sister?" I said in a soft voice: "Carol". Carol eventually wound up going to Eileen George's healing service with her husband -- to David's great surprise.

After that I found that I would pray only sparingly over people in person. I felt comfortable praying over David, because he was in line with the Church. I wasn't sure whether I was being obedient to the Church in praying over people.

Then I was invited to speak at the home of Marianne and John. In prayer I asked Padre Pio's assistance -- whether it would be alright to go speak at this home and witness about my life. My heart said to go, but that if I saw one red light I was going to turn around and go home. To my surprise, every light was green and I found the house without difficulty. Marianne had invited me because of a word of knowledge I gave her the previous week at another prayer group. She asked me to come and share at her house. That was the first time I prayed over a large number of people -- about twenty people at the house. At the end of the prayer time, I sat down and asked for prayer from all the people. When the group started to pray over me, Padre Pio appeared. He was standing before me, slightly bent toward me, with his hands extended and a smile of approval on his face. Marianne looked up and also saw him. She let out a big scream and started telling people what she saw -- which was also what I was looking at. No one else could see him. But many people there could smell the aroma of roses throughout the house. Marianne ran in front of me to explain to the people where the spot was that Pio was standing. I told her to get out of the way. Pio looked at me and then left. I told Marianne and John not to worry, and they asked me to come back the next week. I told them I would pray about it.

I prayed, and the Lord told me to go. I felt that Pio was leading me there again. This time Marianne and John mentioned that they were going on a retreat with Eileen George. I was unable to attend that retreat. Marianne said that she didn't know what to ask Eileen (who at that time was giving everyone five or ten minutes for one-on-one conversation). I told Marianne that, if she couldn't think of anything to ask Eileen, then ask her whether it was okay for me to do what I was doing: namely, coming to her house and teaching. Marianne agreed to ask this question. After her retreat, she called me and told me that I couldn't come unless I had a spiritual director. I agreed that I would no longer come without the benefit of a spiritual director, because I wanted to be obedient to the Church. So Marianne and John stopped holding this prayer group at their house -- because I was unable to come.

A Spiritual Director

Then I started to pursue (through prayer and fasting) the direction of the Lord to seek a spiritual director. I would still occasionally attend prayer groups, including the one at Franklin, where I would pray only with David. As I pursued this course of praying and fasting for a spiritual director, I asked the Lord to let me know if I was taking the right path or the proper approach. Then David showed up at my house unannounced, and started lecturing me about how I needed a spiritual director. I showed him the names of all the priests that I had been putting under a statue of Our Lady of Mound Carmel since the time of Eileen George's advice. I told him that it didn't seem I was being led to any one of those names.

A few weeks passed. In praying with David I mentioned to him that he should pray for the priest he was seeing at BC (Fr. Ron Tacelli, as I later found out) because he was very sick. David gave me a bewildered look, protesting that the priest was not here, he was in Germany, so he (David) wouldn't know whether he (Fr. Tacelli) was sick. But I told David again to pray for him, because he was sick and was coming home. David answered that this couldn't be true, because he had just left and was on a sabbatical, so he wouldn't be right back home. I repeated that he would be. David looked puzzled and left. Shortly thereafter David called me to tell me that he had just seen Fr. Tacelli walking down a corridor in the philosophy department at BC. He told me it was really hard to believe, but Fr. Tacelli had come back due to sickness -- just as David had been told. When David called me in shock and told me that Fr. Tacelli was back home, the Lord said to me: "Frank, he is home for you. You are to go to him." I asked David for his telephone number.

I prayed first for confirmation, asking the Lord to have Fr. Tacelli pick up the phone if I was to go see him. Father did pick up the phone and agreed on an appointment time to see me immediately. I met him at 2 PM, and proceeded to tell him about my life and the things that were happening to me. I told him the story about the word of knowledge to David that he (Fr. Tacelli) was sick and was coming home to direct me. Father looked puzzled, because David had not told him about this episode. (I had presumed that David had told him in advance.) I asked him whether he would agree to be my spiritual director. Then Father asked me a couple of other questions and told me that this would cost me dearly. I myself thought that I would have to pay him money, not knowing what spiritual direction was. But Father eased my mind by telling me that the first thing it was going to cost me was that there would never be a moment in the day when I would not be praying for him. I felt peaceful about that. The next thing was shocking: he asked me to pray over him right then and there. I was very surprised, because David had assured me that he was orthodox; so I assumed he would reject me and I wouldn't have to have anything to do with these things ever again. I thought he would lock me in a closet (so to speak) and I would never have to come out. I was hoping he would think I was a fraud, so I wouldn't have to be bothered with these things anymore. But Father's answer to me after I prayed over him was that he would call me and let me know if he accepted becoming my spiritual director. I asked him what I should do in the meantime. He said to continue what I was doing, but to do it slowly. I was quite surprised when he called me in two days and agreed to be my spiritual director. We have been together now for fifteen years.

Fr. Tacelli assured me that the things I was getting were coming from God. Father told me that whenever I went anywhere and the Lord told me to pray over people I should do it. Since I now had a spiritual director, I was going various places with the permission of the Church. I asked him whether there was anything more I should do, but Father replied that we would work together to see what doors the Lord would open. The first doors that seemed to open were giving retreats for Confirmation programs. Eventually this led to giving talks of witness at prayer groups, giving Life-in-the-Spirit seminars, doing prison ministry, and conducting healing services.

Miscellaneous Healings

Among the healings which the Lord worked in me and through me, I would consider three to be the most impressive. The first one that I will relate was a personal healing. The other two healings involved other people; for these the Lord used me as a channel or an instrument.

The first one would be my own physical healing of high blood-pressure, overweight, and high cholesterol. My arthritis doctor had sent me for a regular physical. The doctor that examined me was a woman who was a fourth-year GP intern. I told her that the reason why I was there was to find out what else could be wrong, because I wanted to ask Jesus to heal whatever else was wrong with me. She diagnosed that I had high blood-pressure, was thirty-three pounds overweight, and my cholesterol was 380. She told me to come back in twenty-nine days, and she would have a program and diet for me to follow. During these twenty-nine days I just prayed and fasted. When I came back she said with amazement: "I see you lost the weight," sarcastically adding: "I suppose the blood-pressure will be normal." I told her to check it out. It was fine. Then she checked the cholesterol. At this point she became very angry. She told me it was impossible for my cholesterol to drop from 380 to 160. She checked it again and it was still 160. She took my medical folder, slammed it down, and said: "I don't want to hear about this Jesus Christ." She then asked me: "May I retain you as a patient when I start my own practice?" I told her she could call me anytime. But she never did.

When I came home, I told my friend Rich (who is a pharmacist) about the incident with the doctor. He informed me that the reason for her anger was that, as a fourth-year intern, she was required to explain the dramatic cholesterol drop in only twenty-nine days. According to Rich, the only way she could have explained this unheard-of occurrence was to use my religious explanation.

At a later time I was awakened at 3 AM, found myself getting dressed, and was in my automobile. When I got in the car, I heard the voice telling me to go to LaSalette. I drove there, and when I arrived I was told to climb the holy stairs up to the crucifix. Everything was black. But to my surprise when I reached the top of the stairs, there was a woman kneeling before the crucifix. I asked her if she wanted a prayer. She agreed. When I prayed with her, I asked her who Zechariah and Jeremiah were. To me they were the names of prophets, but she kindly said that they were her sons. At that point two boys, about eight and nine years of age, stood up from behind a small stone wall. I said to them: "Come on, Mom is going home now." They climbed over the wall and I told them that God had heard their prayer. I knew through a word of knowledge that she wanted to commit suicide. I told the mother that it was through the praying of her two sons that God brought me there. She nodded and said that that was why she was not afraid of me in the dark. After a short conversation, she left with her two children, and then I left. Approximately one month later, I was invited to a Mass in Rhode Island at a prayer group where I met her. She remembered me and thanked me for being obedient to God.

At a still later date, a good friend of mine named Yvon came to my house and asked me to come to a hospital with him in Rhode Island, because his mother Joesphine was very sick and was in intensive care. Upon arriving at the hospital, Yvon heard from his brothers and sisters that the doctors had said that their mother did not have much time left. At that point we went to the desk, where the nurse informed us that we could go in to see her. We proceeded to her room, where we saw that she had every conceivable type of machinery attached to her. Her vital signs were low. I told Yvon I would pray over her and then leave. I began to pray over her, and as I prayed I saw very clearly St. Bernard of Clairvaux in front of me for a brief second. I told Yvon that she was going to be okay and would be upstairs out of intensive care in three days. He told me that he didn't believe this could be true, because his siblings had told him that they were already planning her funeral. At that point the nurse became very angry with me, saying that I was giving a false hope to him; she asked who I was, telling me that Josephine was in very serious condition. Then I left with Yvon. On the way out I told him that his mother had a great devotion to St. Bernard and she would be fine.

In the meantime, a friend of Yvon, who had come with us and who had stayed behind in the waiting area, was approached by Yvon's siblings (all thirteen of them) and was asked whether the man who went into the intensive care room with Yvon was a priest, because they had been waiting all night on watch to get in. (Only two people at a time could enter Josephine's room.) Yvon's friend replied that I was not a priest, but was just a good friend of Yvon.

Three days later Yvon came to pick me up and brought me back to the hospital. We went to the intensive care desk, where he asked for his mother. The nurse at the desk replied that Josephine was in a regular room upstairs. We went up to her room. She spoke French and could not speak English, but she knew I spoke only English. So when she saw me she called out "Saint Bernard!" and extended her hand to me, addressing me "Père" ("Father" in French). She kept repeating these words alternately ("Saint Bernard", "Père"). The reason why she said this was that she had also seen St. Bernard when I had prayed over her, despite the fact that she had been in a comatose state. She told her son Yvon that as a young girl she used to pray to St. Bernard for his intercession and that St. Bernard had appeared to her. Therefore, he came again when I prayed over her. It has been twelve years since this episode, and Josephine is still in good health, having gone back to her normal way of life on the farm in Canada after leaving the hospital.

More Visions of Saints

I want to emphasize that in and of myself I am no better than anyone else. But the Lord in His love and mercy has allowed me to continue teaching with wisdom in discourse, giving me a greater awareness of my angel and permitting me to see various saints. Among these, along with St. Padre Pio and St. Bernard, were St. Jerome, St. Catherine of Siena, and St. Pius X. I will briefly discuss the context of these three apparitions.

The reason I saw St. Jerome was that a woman called me to ask my prayers for getting her three children into parochial school. In praying, I was told by the Lord to tell her to pray to St. Jerome. She informed me that the school had already been in session for nearly a month and she had been told it would be next to impossible to get them all in, but she was hoping to get at least one child in. I reassured her that she should pray to St. Jerome. Later in the day,

another woman called. In prayer, I told her to pray to St. Jerome.
I got a word of knowledge that it had to do with grandchildren.
She said she was trying to get her two grandchildren into Christian
day-care school. I reassured her to pray to St. Jerome. A few days
later both women called back. The younger woman said that all
three children got into the parochial school. The elderly woman
said that she had gotten both her grandchildren into the Christian
day-care center. Yet both women had been told that it would be
impossible. When I arrived for noon Mass at LaSalette that day, I
found out it was the feast of St. Jerome. That night, when I was
praying in thanksgiving to St. Jerome, he appeared, smiled, and left.
(I knew it was him, and this was later confirmed by a painting of
him that I saw.)

I was praying one evening and saw St. Catherine of Siena. I
believed it was her, but wasn't sure. I called Fr. Tacelli and asked
to see him. At our meeting I described her to him and he said that
it sounded like her, but he wasn't sure that St. Catherine had a
crown of thorns (as I had seen in the vision). Father spoke to
another priest, who said that she did not have a crown of thorns. I
was puzzled, because I really thought it was her. When I got home,
Father called and told me that it *was* her, as he found out from
another priest. I understood from this apparition that when I went
out to speak I had to speak boldly, as St. Catherine had done.
When I arrived at a certain prayer group where I had never been
before, the Lord told me that there were six women there who
wanted divorces and that I had to speak out against it -- which I
did. To confirm that everything I did was proper, I asked the Lord
for a word of knowledge to give somebody. There was a young
woman about twenty years old there. I walked over to her and told
her that she had been praying about entering the convent -- trying
to decide between the Franciscans and the Carmelites. I told her to
go to the Carmelites. One of the women who wanted a divorce
jumped up and reported that this was all that this girl had been

praying for. Both were surprised that I knew this, especially the younger woman. I left and never went back, because I had done what I was supposed to do, as St. Catherine had accomplished *her* appointed task.

One day I was having a conversation with an elderly gentleman in my living room. Suddenly I looked up and saw Pope St. Pius X. I looked at the gentleman and said: "You have a devotion to Pius X." He was surprised that I knew that, and he asked me how I knew it. I replied that on the left of him I saw Pius X. Then he said that the reason why he had this devotion was in thanksgiving to this Pope for allowing him to receive Holy Communion at a young age.

✝
Author's Commentary

The preceding narrative ends Frank Kelly's autobiography at the point where he wished to cease speaking in his own words. But his story continues. There is much more to tell than what he, in his reticence, has decided to say. Despite his disability from rheumatoid arthritis and a heart condition, his ministry consisting of healing services, spiritual seminars, and Confirmation instruction classes has gradually expanded from the Eastern regions of the United States into the Midwest. His periods of prayer with individual people are powerfully accentuated by his gift of the discerning word of knowledge -- often accompanied by Scriptural verses personally designated for the recipient of his prayers to the Lord.

Let me offer some commentary, beginning with a few general remarks on so-called "charismatic gifts" (which Frank Kelly prefers to label "apostolic gifts"), followed by an explanation for the title and cover of the book you hold in your hands.

There is no shortage of people skeptical about claims of charismatic gifts -- whether word of knowledge, prophecy, healing, or tongues. In general, this attitude is quite understandable and justified. Indeed, many claims are exaggerated or even counterfeit, and can therefore be fairly readily dismissed. It appears that during most periods of Church history the Holy Spirit does *not* bestow these extraordinary manifestations with widespread profusion. These external phenomena contrast with the internal supernatural gifts of the infused virtues (the theological virtues of faith, hope, and charity, along with the cardinal virtues of prudence, justice, fortitude, and temperance). The latter virtues all regularly accompany (or are increased by) the worthy reception of the

Sacraments -- the ordinary channels through which the Holy Spirit also confers His seven gifts of wisdom, knowledge, understanding, counsel, fortitude, piety, fear of the Lord. (See Isaiah 11:2-3 and *The Catechism of the Catholic Church*, nn. 1803-1832.)

Despite all this, it does *not* follow that the Holy Spirit *never* grants these special charisms in a particular era for the upbuilding of the Church. It simply means that these things will probably be rare, and (in any event) must be tested and discerned by competent ecclesiastical authority, such as a prudent spiritual director. (See the *CCC*, nn. 799-801.) As St. Paul implies in 1 Corinthians 12, these charisms *can* be genuine. In fact, many saints down through the ages have displayed remarkable outward gifts. In our own time, we need only think of St. Padre Pio. Perhaps Frank Kelly shares a portion of the "spirit" of Pio, to whom he has always had a special devotion.

Readers interested in an "official" Catholic exegesis of St. Paul's 1 Corinthians 12-14 are referred to Appendix 1, which reproduces Pope John Paul II's interpretive elaboration on the Pauline discourse. Another trustworthy source is St. Thomas Aquinas, whose writings on this topic I discuss in Appendix 2.

Next, let me comment on the front cover of this book, which depicts Frank Kelly's arthritic hand in the posture he uses when praying over people. In this picture he is also holding rosary beads, amidst a luminous celestial backdrop of white and blue. The scene is shattered by a jagged bolt of yellow lightning on one side, yet softly interrupted by a wide beam of golden light on the other side. This imagery is, of course, symbolic. The lightning bolt striking at his hand signifies Frank's electrocution and the rheumatoid arthritis that flared up in its wake. The broad band of heavenly light illuminating both the rosary beads and his hand represents our Lady's mantle of protection, intervening to spare his life. Perhaps we can accredit this miracle to our Blessed Mother's intercession on account of Frank's devotion to her -- exhibited, in at least one way, by his faithful recitation of her beloved prayer, the Rosary. As Pope John Paul II wrote in 2002 in his Apostolic Letter *Rosarium Virginis Mariae* (*The Rosary of the Virgin Mary*), "The Church has always attributed particular efficacy to this prayer, entrusting to the Rosary, to its choral recitation and to its constant practice, the most difficult problems. At times when Christianity itself seemed under threat, its deliverance was attributed to the power of this prayer, and Our Lady of the Rosary was acclaimed as the one whose intercession brought salvation."

A few remarks on the title and subtitle of the book. The wording (such as "short circuit") should not be casually dismissed as melodramatic hype. As Father Ronald K. Tacelli indicates in his Preface, the spiritual saga of Frank Kelly is, in a very real sense, about electricity.

Electricity is, like fire, paradoxical in nature. Uncontrolled, its intense energy is injurious and destructive. But properly chaneled, it supplies us with the benefits of light and heat. Despite the fact that Frank's body was damaged (yet ultimately saved from utter destruction) by a high-voltage electrical surge, his shocking experience led to his service as a reliable auxiliary (though non-ordained) channel of God's supernatural light and heat -- what we theologically call actual and sanctifying grace. God, in His mysterious providential design, chose to "zap" Frank in a special manner (both literally and figuratively). And Frank has wound up being a good conductor for the current of grace, because through him God has "zapped" others with whom Frank has come into contact.

The motif of the rosary beads fits well here. For they form a chain which, in closing up, is literally a *circuit*. Furthermore, according to such writers on the Blesssed Virgin Mary as St. Louis Grignon de Montfort, St. Alphonsus Liguori, and St. Maximilian Kolbe, true devotion to her is a sure and comparatively speedy route to salvation. A main expression of such devotion is praying her Rosary. Thus, the Rosary becomes a *short* circuit to God. In fact, as Pope John Paul reminds us in his aforementioned Letter on the Rosary, Christ's crucifix is at the core or heart of this circuit.

The Rosary has, moreover, been described as a "lightning rod" -- meaning that, through our Lord's atonement on the cross and our Lady's intercession, mankind can be spared from justly deserved Divine wrath and chastisement. If, however, we focus on the shape of the rosary beads, we might additionally consider them a "lightning chain" -- which also evokes images of the "chain lightning" occurring in some electrical storms. For this reason, the quotation from Bl. Bartolo Longo printed on the Dedication page seems especially relevant.

Now Frank never asked for electrocution (obviously!) nor for the notoriety of his special spiritual ministry marked by certain charisms that later developed. He realizes that of himself he doesn't possess any extraordinary knowledge or power. He is quick to acknowledge that any good accomplished through him is all God's doing (see John 15:5, 2 Corinthians 3:5, and Philippians 2:13). Frank doesn't trumpet Frank. Invoking the Jesuit motto, he constantly reminds those who know him personally: "All for the (greater) glory of God". He goes on outreach only where God's Will sends him. If he had his preference, as he has often said, he would retire like a recluse to some sort of hermitage. (Or even "check out" entirely -- see Philippians 1:19-26.) If he were not continually interrupted by telephone calls and visitors, he would pray virtually all day long in the religious seclusion of home, church, or shrine.

This is precisely why Frank is an apt instrument of the Lord's extraordinary gifts (which, as I noted before, Frank insists on calling "apostolic" rather than "charismatic"). Charisms such as word of knowledge, prophecy, and the healing of other people are spiritually harmful to the degree that pride is present in the soul of the recipient. Most of us would become puffed up if *we* were favored with such Divine manifestations. In practice, we tend to forget the truth of what St. Bernard of Clairvaux wrote: namely, the three fundamental virtues are "humility, humility, and humility". Tempted to pride as we are, we need humility to keep in perspective our limited role in whatever good that the Holy Spirit condescends to accomplish through our God-given talents and our meager efforts.

For all these reasons, *I* (**not** Frank) selected the three Scriptural epigraphs from the books of the prophets Daniel, Isaiah, and Joel. Let me emphasize that Frank Kelly is far too self-effacing to have picked these passages to highlight a book about him. But *I* find them appropriate. Although it is true that he has been shown many signs and wonders (see the Daniel verses) and has been granted visions and a spirit of prophecy (see the Joel verse), what takes center stage is the fact that he has really *heard* the Lord's call (as expressed in the passage from Isaiah). Since he himself is receptive to the word of Divine instruction, he can in turn (with "a learned tongue") teach and encourage others -- those of us who are wearied by the burdens of life in this world and who may suffer from insufficient lack of trust in God's care for us.

It is no coincidence, therefore, that Frank was cured of congenital partial-deafness after he was "zapped". Indeed, this cure seems symbolic. The Lord "opened his ears" in a two-fold sense: physically and spiritually. Thus, he who listened to God ever since childhood -- he who lent God his ears -- would get them back made whole, in order to "listen" ever more intently via the depths of inner locution.

Finally, lest someone accuse me of having the audacity to attempt to write a "hagiography" of someone still alive in this world, I deny the charge on three grounds.

First, without hesitation I profess that only the Pope has the authority to canonize a saint, and that the canonized person must be someone who has departed this earthly life. Now, I am surely *not* the Pope and Frank Kelly is *still* a wayfarer on this planet. (Please stay around for a long time, Frank!)

Second, St. Luke and St. Paul called the ordinary Christians of their time "saints" or "God's holy ones" (see, for example, Acts 9:32,41; 26:10; Romans 8:27; 12:13; 15:25,26,31; 16:2,15; 1 Corinthians 14:33; 16:1,15; 2 Corinthians 1:1; 8:4; 9:1,12; 13:13; Ephesians 1:1,15; 3:8; 4:12; 5:3; 6:18; Philippians 1:1; 4:21,22; Colossians 1:2; etc.). Frank himself sometimes employs this terminology when referring to other members of the Church in apparent good standing within the Mystical Body of Christ.

Third, granted that many people can rightly be called "saints" according to correct Biblical vocabulary and that this author perhaps knows some of them who are even more "saintly" than Frank Kelly, why not write a book about *them*? Well, the point is *not* to canonize *any* of us here below. We (Frank Kelly included) are all still undergoing the great trial. Hence, this book is **not** a "hagiography". Once again, it comes down to a question of the spectacular phenomenon of someone who survived what should have been a lethal dosage of electricity. Why was his life spared? Although there may be other "saints" around who are far holier than Frank Kelly (Frank would be among the first to admit this possibility!), to my knowledge his strange case is locally unique -- undoubtedly by a dispensation of Divine Providence that is evidently for God's glory and our edification. The subsequent events bear out this verdict.

Along with Frank Kelly's spiritual director, Father Ronald Tacelli, I invite the reader to savor the following testimonials. There are about three dozen of them (counting a poetic testimonial honoring Frank in Appendix 3) -- all from those grateful for God's blessings that somehow arrived through the secondary and instrumental causality of Francis B. Kelly.

✝

Testimonials about Frank Kelly

The testimonials of many people who have witnessed the Holy Spirit's charismatic gifts (or "apostolic" gifts, as Frank Kelly prefers to call them) operating through Frank were solicited. These are their personal stories, compiled and presented here with a minimum of editing.

Corroboration about Start of Prayer Ministry

In the mid-1980s Frank Kelly came into my life through the doors of St. Joseph Chapel at St. Mary's Church in Wrentham, Massachusetts. For some unknown reason I had placed a Padre Pio devotional tract behind the small crucifix that hung on the wall close to the door frame. When Frank walked in and saw the devotional tract, to him this was a sign to stay and witness about his life. At this time I don't think that Frank realized the power of God working inside him and the great gifts he would receive.

We have worshiped, prayed, and praised together for many years. I can remember at one point in my life when, due to an occupational hazard, my hands and wrists developed Carpel Tunnel Syndrome. Attending the prayer meeting in Wrentham, Frank saw my hands in braces and said: "Let me pray with you." He stated: "In six weeks you will receive a healing." During this time I was under the care of Dr. Sands, an orthopedic surgeon at a Norwood facility, where he thought surgery might be the answer. I waited six weeks and was able to throw the braces away. Praise God.

Frank has been blessed with a unique way in which to pray

over God's chosen ones. He prays over a person in the spirit of tongues and always leaves you with a word of knowledge about whom to pray to (perhaps our Blessed Mother Mary or a particular saint) and also Scripture readings which coincide with each other -- sending one home with much to think and pray about, thus igniting the Spirit of God within that individual person.

Approximately seven years ago, Frank approached me, as he usually does when seeing me, and prayed. He asked whether my husband was thinking of purchasing any real estate. My reply was: "I don't think so." Well -- lo and behold -- shortly after this, our family business bought a parcel of land, which was blessed by Fr. John Fernz. Today our own family business facility resides on the property. Again, praise God.

Through the years Frank has touched many of my family members and friends. My sister Lynda has truly been affected by Frank, not only watching Frank's healings and prophecies unfold, but also through his teachings. His teaching abilities come from God, because knowing Frank for as many years as I have, I can say that in no way do they come from him. He is able to teach humbly, with excitement in a simple holy fashion, while keeping within the laws of the Roman Catholic Church. Placing his total trust in Almighty God, he affects people with God's love and projects an awesome spirit of humor, which relaxes people so that they are comfortable knowing there is a God who loves them and cares.

(Phyllis Gamble)

Personal Witness of Padre Pio Vision

One night, about twelve years ago, we had a Rosary group at my house. After the Rosary, Frank Kelly was praying over us all. When he came to me, he and I together saw Padre Pio in my living room. He was bent over a little and had a beautiful smile on his face. He was only there for a moment. I got so excited, I yelled. Frank said I scared him away. Maybe I did, but we *did* see him.

(Marianne Sarnie)

Another Corroboration of Vision and St. Thérèse

A certain night when we were at my daughter Marianne's house, Frank Kelly was praying over the people there. All of a sudden Marianne started screaming. Both she and Frank saw Padre Pio at the same time.

Frank prayed over me that night, even though I was skeptical about it. He mentioned the name "Tom" to me. I was startled, because that's the name of my deceased brother. I told Frank that Tom was my brother's name, but he was dead. Frank replied that he knew, and that Tom was in heaven, because the intercession of St. Thérèse got him there. This was remarkable, because Tom did have a devotion to St. Thérèse. (Coincidentally, his last name and my maiden name is the same as St. Thérèse's family name -- Martin.)

I never believed before this episode about people being prayed over, but now I know that Frank is for real after what happened that night.

(Mary Teague)

Corroboration of Sudden Cure of Deafness

In order to share with you about how Frank Kelly came into my life, I first have to tell you a little about my life.

My husband died young, and about a year after his death I left the Church. My life went from bad to worse. About ten years later, I made a Life in the Spirit seminar. That is when I met Frank. The seminar brought me back to the Church, as the Holy Spirit changed my life. After being away so long, I had many struggles. Frank answered many of my questions and encouraged me, as did the other members of the prayer group I had joined.

I had seen Eileen George in a couple of other churches. I knew that Frank went to Worcester often to see her. I had never felt drawn to go, until one Sunday. I called Frank to see whether I could go with him. Another person was supposed to go also. After many phone calls, we finally got it set, so off we went a little late. Eileen would give her talk, and then would walk the aisles and call out healings. She started up the aisle where we were seated, and she kept looking at me. I wondered what she was going to say, and then she looked at Frank. She pointed to him and said that the Lord had healed his ears. Frank immediately took out both hearing aids. I looked at his ears, and they were bright red. When we got outside, I touched one of his ears, and it was red hot. Now I understand why I felt the need to go that day. Because Frank had helped me so much, the Lord allowed me to witness his healing.

One time we were driving home from a prayer meeting, and Frank said: "The Lord doesn't want you to remarry." I had dated for a number of years, but did not find love. Some of my widowed friends had remarried, and I had wondered why I had not found anybody to love. Now I had my answer.

Another time he told me that my husband was praying for me. I'm sure that my saintly mother, who had been dead for years, was also praying for me, and that these prayers brought me back to the Church.

One night at the prayer meeting, I had an infection in my eye. I asked Frank to pray over it. He told me there was a reason why the Lord allowed it. As the eye did not improve, I went to the doctor. In looking in my eye, he discovered that my eyes were yellow, so he sent me for a liver scan, which was fine. But it turned out that one of my medications was causing the problem. Frank was right. If I hadn't had the eye infection, my liver could have been damaged before it was detected.

Another time some members of my prayer group were praying with me. Frank said that he didn't know I had a bad back. I told him I had had it since I was young. He said that the Lord had told him to pray for my back. I stood up and he did. My back has never been healed, even though may priests and many laypeople have prayed for it. But I'm sure that the prayers have kept it from being worse than it is, and it doesn't slow me down much.

Many times when Frank is praying in church, someone would admire his rosary beads. Even if it was a pair he really liked, he would give them away.

God has placed so many wonderful people in my life to help me in my journey. Frank has so many gifts that he helped me very much.

(Carmelita Ward)

Mighty Gifts from God

Our Lady of Hope Prayer Group in Franklin is the common link between Frank Kelly and myself. For me, it began in the early 1990s. Reflecting on those times, I remember that the Spirit of God was sent into a whirlwind when Frank would appear. At the end of our prayer meetings, I observed Frank praying with members of our group, sharing prophecies and healings. Then the next week I would hear of a confirmation. What mighty gifts the Lord has bestowed upon Frank.

64

The spiritual grapevine between Frank, my sister Phyllis, our dearly departed friend Rheta, and myself was a strong bond. Each of us was affected by his teachings. Many of them happened over the telephone -- it had become our spiritual hot-line. There were also many talks over coffee leading into hours of teachings. Frank has such power under such humility, teaching us to open our eyes to see the wonders around us and the truths that will set us free.

Frank was always testing us with questions, stimulating our minds and hearts to get our spirit moving in the right direction. There is one question that will remain with me always: "Who is God???". Through his teachings and his direction to many Biblical passages, I was able to handle many personal situations with my loved ones. Frank taught me to act, not react, with the love of Jesus; and many fruits of the Spirit poured forth with the great peace of God.

Frank has a single-hearted zeal and a gentle wisdom. He has directed many people to find God by using devotions and prayer, learning to overcome our tension and fears, and replacing them with trust and the search for peace. Frank is open to everyone any time, even in the middle of the night -- people asking for prayer. He is there willing to pray and help in any way.

I have made great steps forward in my walk with the Lord due to Frank's teachings and prayers. The devotion to our Blessed Lady Mary has become alive in my life, and I owe this to Frank's teachings too. I have learned to trust God unconditionally.

(Lynda Embree)

Academics and Weight Gain

I have been marginally involved with the Catholic "charismatic movement" since 1976, when I first made a "Life-in-the-Spirit" seminar at the Newman Center on the campus of the University of Massachusetts (where I was a graduate student in mathematics). Since then I have been an off-and-on participant in this "movement", though a regular observer of the local Catholic charismatic scene. (I have refused to become involved with any so-called "charismatic" group that is not authentically Catholic -- which means, according to my perspective, that it cannot tolerate dissent from Catholic doctrine and it must hold in high esteem the Holy Sacrifice of the Mass as well as traditional Catholic devotions, such as the Rosary.)

Years before I ever heard of Frank Kelly, I used to pray that someday I would meet someone with miraculous gifts. Well, I guess this prayer was answered. For in all the years since my introduction to the Catholic charismatic movement, I have never encountered anyone with such pronounced extraordinary gifts from God as Frank.

I have far too many stories to relate of remarkable personal incidents connected with Frank; I doubt that a whole book would suffice to contain them all. Therefore, I will recount only the most outstanding ones. Moreover, I will try to indicate which episodes concerned his charism of the word of knowledge and which concerned his charism of prophecy. I am aware from reading other testimonials that he may have a charism of healing, but the word of knowledge and prophecy seem more pertinent to my case in dealing with him.

It was around 1986 or 1987 when I first met Frank. I used to see him mainly at St. Mary's church in Franklin after the Wednesday evening Mass sponsored by Our Lady of Hope prayer group, although I also ran into him a couple of times at Our Lady of LaSalette Shrine in Attleboro.

During the years from 1985 to 1992 I was a PhD. candidate in philosophy at Boston College, taking graduate courses from

1985 to 1988 and teaching introductory undergraduate classes from 1986 to 1992. Between 1988 and 1993 I taught courses on the philosophy of St. Thomas Aquinas at Our Lady of Grace minor seminary college run by the Oblates of the Virgin Mary in Boston, and from 1989 to 1996 I taught similar courses at the House of Studies run by the Daughters of St. Paul in Boston. So there were several academic years (namely, 1989 to 1992) during which I was teaching simultaneously at all three schools (three part-time positions). Along with this teaching, I was playing the organ for the choir at Our Lady of Fatima Shrine in Holliston twice weekly, as well as for our parish prayer group's weekly Mass. I was also involved in our parish's Respect for Life Committee. I felt much stress from being so incredibly busy.

Well, Frank would pray over me and get a word of knowledge initially in the form of a question: "Where are the fruits?" I was flabbergasted by such a rude question, because it seemed that there were plenty of fruits in my work. I replied more than once: "What do you mean: Where are the fruits?" Yet he persisted in dogging me with this nagging question. But his word of knowledge didn't remain at the interrogatory level; it was accompanied by a declarative word of knowledge. He explained: "You're doing everything but the one thing God wants you to do." I asked him what that was. He replied: "You're supposed to be getting your doctorate." I knew what that meant, because I had been continuously postponing writing my doctoral dissertation. For one thing, I doubted my ability to do it, and only gave myself a fifty percent chance of ever writing an acceptable Ph.D. thesis. Anyway, although I had done much of the background research, I never seemed to have the time to begin the actual writing. Frank predicted that things would work out and that I would get the opportunity to write it.

It turned out that I was awarded a dissertation fellowship for the 1992-1993 academic year, during which period I was relieved from my undergraduate teaching duties at Boston College and paid to write my thesis. Although I did continue to teach that year at the Oblates of the Virgin Mary seminary and the Daughters of St. Paul House of Studies, I had so few students altogether that there was hardly any work entailed. Thus, I finally did have enough time to write my dissertation---- which I churned out from July, 1992, to March, 1993. I publicly defended my thesis on the feast of St. Joseph, March 19. I have to give Frank credit for goading me with his words of knowledge and his accurate prophecy; otherwise, I'm not sure whether I would ever have obtained the Ph.D. degree in philosophy. Of course, while engaged in writing this book (titled *Matter, Physical Quantity, and Place in Scholastic Cosmology: The Influence of Eucharistic and Eschatological Physics*) my heavenly patron was St. Thomas Aquinas.

As remarkable as this whole prolonged experience was, it pales in comparison with what happened next. Since I was so nervous on the day of my doctoral defense, Frank drove me into Boston College and was present in the room along with my dissertation director (Prof. Norman Wells), my second reader (Fr. Ron Tacelli), the department chairman (Fr. Joseph Flanagan), my spiritual director (Fr. Raymond Fournier), and several other people (Prof. Oliva Blanchette, Fr. Pius Devoti from Fatima Shrine, and a couple of graduate students). After the affair was over and we were back in Frank's car, the first thing he said to me was: "Now you have to write one in math." I was utterly astounded, for several reasons.

First, the preceding December (1992) I had been wondering what I should do upon graduation from B.C., especially if I didn't get a teaching position in philosophy. At that time Frank had prayed over me and prophesied that within three weeks I would know what to do. Sure enough, by mid-January I realized that I should hedge my bets. In case I didn't get a full-time teaching

68

position in philosophy, I ought to play it safe and tie up some loose ends by returning to graduate school in mathematics. I already had a master's degree in math. from B.C. (1974) and had spent an additional two years enrolled in a doctoral program in math. at the University of Massachusetts in Amherst (1975-1977). But I never completed the Ph.D. degree in mathematics; for one thing, I doubted my ability to write an original research thesis. At any rate, despite this previous drop-out, I decided (as a Plan B in case Plan A didn't work out) to seek entrance once again to a doctoral program in mathematics. In January, 1993, I applied to the only graduate school with a Ph.D. program in mathematics that was easily accessible geographically and where I thought I had a good chance of being accepted with a teaching assistantship: namely, Northeastern University. However, I did not tell Frank about my application. So I was startled when on March 19 he brought up this issue. He did not know that two months earlier I had already applied to enroll in a Ph.D. program in mathematics.

Second, even though I did apply to Northeastern, it was more of a lark than anything else -- just an interesting fall-back position in case Plan A failed and I couldn't find a regular teaching job in philosophy. I still didn't think I had the ability to actually finish the degree requirements by writing an acceptable dissertation in mathematics. So when Frank implicitly prophesied that I would do it (a prophecy that he would explicitly repeat many times over the next three or four years), I was amazed and somewhat incredulous.

Third, I was struck by the audacious bluntness of his new pronouncement about my life-- only minutes after the climax of several years of hounding me about the philosophy dissertation. You would think he would have congratulated me and let me rest on my laurels (for a few days at least), instead of starting right up again by getting on my case. If it had been anyone else, I might have been tempted to snap back with something like: "You have a nerve!" or "Have you been snooping into my private affairs?". But I guess I knew deep down inside that what he was saying was so strangely improbable it must have come from God. So I merely said something like: "What? How can you *say* that? How did you know that I've *already* applied for admission to a math. Ph.D. program?" I think he replied to the effect that he knew it from prayer -- a definite word of knowledge and a tacit prediction that my Plan A would fail (i.e., I would not be able to obtain a full-time position teaching philosophy).

Then another odd thing occurred. When Frank dropped me off at my house that evening and I looked through my mail, lo and behold -- there was a letter of acceptance from Northeastern University. I wasn't expecting to hear from them so soon -- not until after April 15, which was the deadline for applications. I figured their admissions committee would wait until then before informing *anyone* about their decision. Of course, I quickly called Frank and told him what had just happened, but he didn't seem at all surprised.

As events turned out, I was able to keep my part-time job teaching philosophy at the Daughters of St. Paul House of Studies, but I did not succeed in securing a full-time position in philosophy. Therefore, I wound up enrolling in the doctoral program in mathematics at Northeastern. I had a very stressful time there, often being tempted to leave the program on account of doubts about my mathematical ability. (As everyone knows, mathematics is a notoriously technical and conceptually challenging discipline, an especially abstract subject at the graduate level -- much more difficult than philosophy.) But Frank warned me that I should just make up my mind to stay with it, because I would have to do it sooner or later -- I was not going to be let off the hook. He encouraged me with prophecies that I *would* pass the required qualifying exams, and that I *would* succeed in writing an acceptable thesis. (I had given myself barely a five percent chance of writing anything more than a page that was mathematically intelligible and original.) Over and again he got the word of knowledge that I should keep praying to St. Albert the Great (the philosopher-theologian-scientist teacher of St. Thomas Aquinas) for his intercession -- which I did. I believe it was through St. Albert's help that I conceived my maverick thesis topic (confirmed by a certain friend) and that I was able to follow through successfully on it. I was constantly experiencing illumination to clear away obscurities encountered. (Frank would also get words of knowledge about how my advisor/ dissertation director was reacting internally to my progress.) Frank even predicted that I would finish all my degree requirements (the last and major hurdle being the dissertation) during my fourth year at Northeastern (1996-1997). I did, passing my dissertation defense on April 25, 1997, and graduating in June, 1997, with a Ph.D. in mathematics. To this day I can still hardly believe it, because (as I said) higher mathematics is far more abstruse than philosophy (which is usually somewhat down to earth in terms of meaningfulness for human existence).

Here is a curious occurrence, but one that seems typical for Frank. One evening during the year of my philosophy dissertation fellowship at Boston College (1992 or 1993), Frank prayed over me and got a word of knowledge or a prophecy that I would be asked to give a talk somewhere. I left the church and went home. Very shortly thereafter, I got a telephone call from Professor Peter Kreeft asking me to deliver a lecture on the angels to one of his classes at B.C. I could not believe it! The phone call came about forty-five minutes after Frank's prediction. Talk about timing! I ran back to the church to tell Frank, who (if I recall correctly) was still there. A skeptic would label this mere coincidence. Well, such so-called "coincidences" are common fare with Frank Kelly.

Another interesting tale straddles (like the above story) the line between a word of knowledge and a prophecy. I think I was still at Northeastern when this took place (probably in 1996 or 1997). After Frank returned from a trip to the upstate New York and Pennsylvania area (where incidentally he encountered a Catholic church named for St. Albert the Great), he told me either that I was going to write a book or that I was supposed to write a book (I forget exactly how he phrased it). I responded that I had already written one: my 320-page philosophy dissertation. Obviously, though, he meant another one -- one that would be commercially published, I suppose. But I dismissed the whole notion with the comment that I had no idea what to write a book about. (I felt that I had nothing more to say and that no publisher would be interested in anything I might write.)

Well, in early 2001 a controversy erupted in the Boston Archdiocese over the problem of celiac disease (allergic intolerance to wheat gluten) and the composition of altar bread for the Holy Eucharist. When the Cardinal was asked to permit substitution of a non-glutinous grain (such as rice cakes) for wheat bread, he refused to grant a dispensation from the traditional practice. This caused an uproar in the media, a forum in which the Church was accused of the usual charges of lacking "compassion" and being "rigid" and "judgmental". But I began to wonder why the Church cannot make exceptions in the valid matter of the sacraments. My research turned into an apologetics book titled *Why Matter Matters: Philosophical and Scriptural Reflections on the Sacraments*, which Our Sunday Visitor agreed to publish in 2002 (with a Foreword by Father Ronald Tacelli and a Preface by Peter Kreeft). Chalk up another one for Frank!

Strangely, when he first foretold to me that I was going to write a book and I replied that I had no idea what to write about, he mentioned (or seemed to suggest) that it could be about him. It turned out that I would write *two* books: one on the matter of the Sacraments and a second one on him! I take this to be a double fulfillment of a prophecy that initially appeared obscure.

So much for academic affairs and on to other weighty matters. A problem I had been tormented with for decades was my inability to gain weight. I had been skinny and scrawny ever since boyhood. Some of my peers (and later, as an adult teaching school, some of my own male students) let me know it in no uncertain terms. It hurt a great deal. Frank would pray over me and "get" that my appetite would improve. This puzzled me, because my appetite was fine; it was my power of digestive assimilation that was deranged. But I figured that's roughly what he meant. (When it comes to private revelation, the word of the Lord does not always pass through the prophet's mouth completely undistorted.) Anyway, in January of 1993 he prophesied that "soon" I would be able to eat ice cream. This was odd, because I had called him on the phone for a totally unrelated purpose; anyway, it was dead winter and I had no desire at that time to eat ice cream. Furthermore, when I had tried to eat ice cream in the past, it had had some bad physical effects on me. I resisted even attempting to eat ice cream until the summer of 1994, when another prayerful friend (Brian B.) urged me to try it. I did and there were no adverse effects, but I stopped eating it regularly out of fear. So I gained no weight from these tentative efforts.

But when the summer of 1995 came around, I decided to throw caution to the wind. I began eating large amounts of Breyer's all-natural ice cream along with doughnuts (another item on Frank's word-of-knowledge grocery list for me). To my astonishment, by the end of the year I had gained twelve pounds, and then a total of fifteen pounds by April of 1996. But I began feeling exhausted all the time and had no idea why. Frank told me he was getting in prayer that I was anemic and should start eating beef. Well, the very idea struck me as absurd, since I had been mostly vegetarian for fourteen years (strictly on account of health concerns, not due to any so-called "animal rights" issues). In fact, the last time I had tried eating beef (in 1982) I had experienced severe intestinal pain. Nevertheless, because Frank insisted on the importance of it for curing my anemia and for putting on even more weight, I finally relented. It turned out, despite my anxious apprehension (which *should* have caused psychosomatic pain), that I had no trouble digesting it. My fatigue vanished and I continued to gain more weight. By October, 1996, I had gained an unprecedented total of twenty-seven pounds -- in only sixteen months. (Later the total would rise to thirty-plus pounds.) To me this was an outright miracle -- all due to Frank's words of knowledge and accompanying prophecies about the efficacy of my adherence to his charismatic counsel. Those skeptics who don't know about the idiosyncracies of my physiological system may attribute the dramatic change to a psychological placebo effect. That's their prerogative. But it would have had to be a very powerful placebo -- just as efficacious as the "real thing" (whatever that might be). Let's have more of these "fake" cures in the arsenal and annals of medical remedies! Hence, given my history of difficulties in metabolizing food properly, I hope that even the die-hard skeptic will understand why I still claim this "healing" bordered on the miraculous.

Many other times (too numerous to detail) Frank would get a word of knowledge about what I should eat or drink or otherwise use to counteract a physical complaint. Usually, the foods and drinks were things I once avoided out of fear: pekoe (rather than herbal) tea, orange juice (which had been too acidic for me to tolerate), and bananas (which formerly produced an allergic reaction) come to mind as current staples. But he would occasionally tell me to eat a rare item not necessarily to be repeated, such as scrambled eggs. Indeed, when I would go overboard in eating such foods, I would pay for it with a distressing reaction. This was even more true of foods (such as chocolate and cheese) that I indulged in on my own with no prior word of knowledge from Frank. Someone may accuse me of being too dependent on Frank's seal of approval (yes, I know what you are thinking). Yet *I* say that you have no right to judge, given my cluelessness about what to eat and drink -- despite years of relying on my own independent resources by studying books on nutrition. I feel that Frank has been an inexpressible blessing in this area, for which I am immensely grateful to God after my many years of floundering with futile visits to physicians (whether mainstream or holistic) and with endless auto-analysis. Moreover, his advice has saved me some money; maybe he should charge fees for such consultations.

But I had a couple of health problems about which Frank *did* advise me to see a physician. Both times the treatment was at least helpful or even successful. The second time (years after the first episode) he told me to pray to St. Camillus de Lellis for his intercession in locating the right physician to help me. The next morning the second doctor whom I called answered the phone himself, and very kindly made an appointment for me to see him that very evening. Although he recommended I come back, the condition cleared up, so I didn't need the follow-up visit.

Then there are the many words of knowledge and prophecies regarding other people about whom I would ask Frank to pray (in person or over the telephone). Nearly always he would be accurate, but obviously I can't share most of these confidential things about relatives and friends. On one occasion (February, 1990), though, he told me that my mother was sick, which was not obvious at the time. But, sure enough, one or two months later she developed the overt clinical symptoms of pneumonia. Thank God she recovered.

Another such (and even more amazing) episode that can be mentioned stands out. When my own regular spiritual director, Father Raymond Fournier, was transferred to a Vermont parish temporarily around 1989, I asked Father Ron Tacelli to serve as my spiritual director for that year. The following summer (I believe it was in July, 1990), Fr. Tacelli left for a sabbatical in Germany and was not expected to return to B.C. during the Fall. Frank prayed over me one evening (I think in August or at the latest in September) and got a word of knowledge that Fr. Tacelli was sick. (Frank may also have said that he would be coming back home to Boston.) I replied that that was impossible; he had just recently left for Europe and was fine. Well, lo and behold, shortly thereafter (perhaps in early October) I met Fr. Tacelli walking down a corridor of the B.C. building where the philosophy department was housed. I asked him what he was doing back in Boston so soon. He responded that he had contracted an infection from a botched root canal and had to return to the States for proper medical treatment. Needless to say, I was thoroughly stupefied. I certainly reported this incident immediately to Frank himself. I didn't think I should tell Father Tacelli about the connection with Frank Kelly at that time, but later on Father found out the whole bizarre story. I do remember telling Father that there was a "loose cannon" praying over people in my area of Massachusetts (a guy who needed a spiritual director), but I don't exactly recall whether I mentioned this fact to Father before or after his aborted sabbatical leave. (I believe it was some time during the previous academic year when I first told him very briefly about Frank Kelly.)

Sometimes when Frank prays over me (perhaps this is true for other people, too), I feel a surge of "power" or "energy" emanating from him -- though not a charge as from an electrical current. Even though his hands need not be touching my head, I feel like falling backward, but I generally resist. *Not* because I am refusing an offer of healing by the Holy Spirit (though this may understandably appear to be the case from the perspective of external observers), but rather because I am afraid that the sensation of wanting to fall backwards stems from my own inner emotional state. I therefore try to "test" the impulse by counteracting the feelings, even if the effort requires intermittent teetering and rocking on my feet. I can't help it that it must look strange to anyone who happens to be around.

Another striking aspect of Frank's gifts. Often when he prays he "gets" pertinent Scripture passages, not knowing what these verses say in advance. When I then read them to him, he can often interpret and apply them appropriately in light of the prayer request at hand. (Frequently a certain friend can give a reasonable exegesis of my readings from Frank.) Sometimes, though, it is hard to see the relevance, because a passage may be construed as universally (or at least generally) applicable. (My friend claims that *his* readings from Frank always tend towards generic platitudes lacking the specificity he is seeking for himself.) Yet even *then* there can be something remarkable, because Frank may cite a book of the Bible with a chapter number and verse numbers where the final number he gives is exactly the last verse of that chapter. In other words, one number higher and the verse could not belong to that chapter. Yet this possibility of a numbering error, which theoretically may cast doubt on (or raise questions about) the authenticity of Frank's gift of Scriptural word of knowledge, has never once materialized in my years of dealing with him.

Someone may claim that Frank's gift of word of knowledge is merely a preternatural psychic phenomenon resulting from his electrocution. But I doubt it. Frank's devotion to the three Persons of the Holy Trinity, to our Blessed Mother Mary, to the angels and the saints, as well as the spiritual fruits of Frank's ministry (which include conversions to the one, holy, Catholic, and Apostolic Church), all leave me convinced that the finger of God points firmly at this man.

It sometimes seems to me that Frank is like Moses: he asks God questions and gets audible replies. Disappointingly, though, a major long-standing prediction of Frank concerning a future job for me has still not come true as of this writing (late Spring/early summer 2002, revised late Spring 2005). But I keep hoping.

Maybe it will happen in the near future.

(David P. Lang)

Lost, Found, and Never Give Up

Dear Brothers and Sisters in Christ:

Don't ever stop thanking, praising, and loving Almighty God with your whole heart and soul. [Some time ago] my daughter Stella, who is a travel agent, left on a trip to Barbados. Upon arriving there she called home, saying those dreaded words: "I lost my wallet with money, credit cards, driver's license, health card, etc." She asked for help on what to do, and also asked us to look around here just in case she misplaced or dropped her wallet while packing. Her father and I searched all over with zero results. Then remembering a similar time when our brother Henry lost his pay-check and called Frank Kelly for help with prayers that his check would be found, of course Almighty God took charge and through Frank and his prayers Henry found the check. Praise God!

Well, you guessed it, I myself called Frank with a similar request for prayers. Frank told me to hang up, say three Hail Mary's (or better still, the whole Rosary) while he prayed. One hour later Frank called, saying that he didn't seem to think Stella's wallet was stolen or lost; he somehow felt that an exchange in luggage resulted while Stella was packing. And you know what.... After searching two days, my [husband] Louie, by accident, hit one of her pocketbooks and -- lo and behold -- he opened it and there was Stella's billfold, all intact. We started to praise God and didn't stop, and we are still praising and thanking Him for all He does for us and all He is going to do.

Praise God. I called Frank. It was quite late, but I did want him to know that his prayers with God's help found my daughter's missing wallet. Frank was out somewhere doing God's work, but I did leave a message with his son, Joseph.

So my dear friends, never give up, no matter what. God is always near us, and even in my illness of cancer I know He's near and holding me in His everlasting Holy Hands. Every night I place an empty chair next to me, and I know Jesus is sitting there in love for me. Thank you.

(† Rheta Frascotti)

Lost and Found, Etc.

I have known Frank Kelly for many years. One time I misplaced my paycheck and panicked. I called Frank to pray with me for the Lord to help me find the check. Frank asked for the intercession of St. Anthony to find the check. After praying for a minute, he told me that the check was in my car. So I went and searched inside the car but couldn't find the check. I again panicked and called Frank back. He prayed some more and then said that the check was behind the seat. I looked again and there it was!

I could tell many other similar stories in connection with Frank concerning many other needs in my life.

(Name Withheld)

Don't Have to Give Up "Everything"

I met Frank in 1989 at the Life in the Spirit Seminar in Franklin. Jim Merski and I were working together at the time and Jim knew that I was having some personal difficulties, so he asked me if I wanted to attend. I told him that I would think about going. The week before the seminar I had a lot of anxiety. I kept thinking that if I got involved with a prayer group I would have to give away every thing I owned (the only Bible passage that I remembered was the one that said if you want to follow Me you have to give up everything). That thought kept running through my head for almost the entire week -- it wouldn't go away.

I finally decided to go, mainly because my brother was struggling with an illness and I thought that maybe I could come to terms with his situation. At the end of the first presentation people were gathering in the back for prayer with Frank. I'm not sure I even wanted him to pray over me, but I was intrigued enough to say okay. When he prayed over me, not only did I have a real sense of peace, but he said that I didn't have to give up anything and that my brother would see some improvement. I was absolutely dumbfounded -- I didn't even know him and yet he addressed the two major concerns of my life at that time. That's all it took for me -- I knew that something big had just happened, and I've been on a thirteen year journey committed to improving my relationship with God and helping other people try to understand the peace you can find when you find God in your life.

(Dorene Christie)

Proper Guidance

I have known Frank Kelly for about thirteen years. There have been many situations where he has prayed with me and through prayer was able to tell me things and guide me in the right direction.

For example, one of the instances was when I was dating a guy and it was a very unhealthy relationship. I had called Frank for prayer and he prayed with me. He told me that this guy was also involved with another girl and that she had previously had an abortion. Needless to say, it all came out in the wash and he *was* dating another girl. Also, Frank told me that he was into drugs, steroids. He was a body-builder who owned his own gym. I found out that, not only was he taking drugs through injection, but he was also dealing them.

Many times Frank has told me stuff that only God would know. When I was pregnant with my daughter, my first child, Frank prayed with me and told me it was a girl. With my second pregnancy, he told me that it was a boy, and we just recently had a healthy baby boy.

A lot of times I will call for prayer and Frank prays over the phone and gives me a reading to read from the Bible. It is unbelievable how the Scriptures are related to what I am asking for.

(Kathy Cogan)

Prophecy of Return and Padre Pio

I met Frank Kelly in January, 1996, at a friend's house in Malden, Massachusetts. While I was there, Frank imposed his hands over each person's head and prayed for that person. He also prayed over me, giving me a chapter and a verse from a certain book of the Holy Scriptures. He also told me something was going to happen to me during my vacation in Brazil.

During the summer of 1997 when Frank and some friends came to Europe for a pilgrimage, I had the occasion to talk to him and get to know him better. While we were visiting the shrines and the sights of Rome, Frank seemed to me to be a pious and simple person, transmitting peace and serenity to all those whom he met and talked with. For me he also seemed to be a person with a real prayer life. He was always praying his Rosary, and his conversation was about God and all matters regarding our Catholic doctrine.

I noticed that Frank does not have excellent health, because he suffers from rheumatoid arthritis. I also noticed several times that he prayed over those who were with him. There is a specific episode that impressed me deeply.

I had just said Mass at Padre Pio's tomb in San Giovanni Rotondo (the monastery where Fr. Pio lived, built a shrine to our Lady, and is buried). Right after the celebration, while I was coming from the sacristy, Frank came close to me. I asked him to say a prayer for me, and he, as usual, recollecting himself and laying his hands on my head, said something in silence. Then he told me: "You will come back to us." (I understood that he meant the U.S.A.)

I was wondering about this sentence, and then I told myself: "That's ridiculous, I'm here in Italy, I intend to go for my master's degree, and what could this possibly mean?" Before I finished my master's in systematic theology in Rome, I had previously asked my bishop whether I could come to North America (U.S.A. or Canada) to help the order of Scalabrinian Fathers as an associated priest. My intention was to help the new migrants in North America, especially "my people -- Brazilians".

After receiving my master's in the summer of 2000, I made arrangements to depart from Italy, where I had been for almost twelve years. My bishop readily gave me permission to begin this new missionary experience. After all the bureaucratic procedures that are required by our Church, I finally had my new destination from the Provincial of the Scalabrinian order, which is located in New York City. I had been assigned to Everett, a small city close to Malden, the place where I had originally met Frank and his friends.

When I left Italy, I first went to Brazil to spend some time with my family, and later I flew to New York City to the provincial house. My big surprise occurred when the provincial Father drove me to my new assignment in Everett. I was to be the parochial vicar for St. Anthony Parish. When we arrived at the church, I noticed on the lawn a big bronze statue of Padre Pio! Now, are all these events connected to the far episode of that summer in 1997 at Fr. Pio's tomb? "You will come back to us"!!! I believe so!

Even now I entrust to Frank, in a very special way, intentions of prayers for relatives or friends who carry heavy burdens. This is what I can personally testify about Mr. Frank Kelly, who is, in my opinion, a good, humble, simple person with a special gift from the Lord.

(Fr. Antonio Carvalho)

Deep Impact on Spiritual Life through Gifts

This is a review of the impact that Frank Kelly has had on my spiritual life.

I met Frank after the 50th Anniversary Mass for Father Edward McDonough in the summer of 1997. The Mass took place in a Watertown Catholic school hall where prayer meetings were frequently held. I arrived late for the service and saw my cousin Bill playing the piano. At this point in my life I was a Catholic in name only and had been slowly returning to my faith. I was unsettled by the number of people at the service and not recognizing anyone inside besides my cousin. I kept walking in and out of the hall. The truth is that I wanted to leave, but Bill had told me that a man he had previously met with special gifts could be there. I was interested in finding out what these gifts could be and where they might help me. I was hungry for a relationship with God.

I finally went and stayed inside and grabbed Bill at the end of the Mass. He pointed out to me an ordinary-looking man who was praying over people, and said: "He's right there." I had previously experienced resting in the spirit from being prayed over by both laypeople and clergy. I was catching people as they rested. Then it became my turn.

Frank started praying and stopped immediately. He said: "God says that you are very anxious and that He doesn't want you to be anxious." I thought, "How does he know this?" and wanted to run, but I felt comfortable with Frank. He started praying again and told me to read Psalm 119 and try to take it easy. He gave me his phone number and told me that I could call him anytime if I had questions. I took him up on his offer and have called him too many times to count.

I was relearning my religious beliefs and Frank was slowly bringing me up to speed. I took note. His gifts are more far-reaching than I will know on this earth. One thing that I know is that he is committed to God's will. He has torn down the punishing ruler that I feared as a child. He showed me a loving God who wants to bless me in a special way. "Jesus our Brother, Mary our Mother, and a great outpouring of the Holy Spirit" have been the consistent lead-off to his prayer in the hundreds of times that we have petitioned God together. He showed me that God doesn't charge money for miracles. He has showed me first-hand what obedience to God can do in our lives through *his* life. He also has a sense of humor, which comes in handy when I start looking for immediate results from God.

It is difficult to describe all of the major and minor things that Frank has helped me get through. My daughter Jennifer was diagnosed with cerebral palsy in 1997. He prayed with me to St. Luke, both before and after the visit to Children's Hospital. He said that God wasn't done with Jennifer yet, and many terrific people (doctors, therapists, and teachers) continue to be part of her life, to the point where she is in the mainstream of school and will enter into first grade next year. She is "light years" ahead of where I would have imagined. I felt secure from the beginning that things would be okay.

Frank's great devotion to Padre Pio and all of the saints, along with the Life in the Spirit seminars, have assisted in my spiritual growth. It brings great emotion to me as I attempt to put the "right words" on the page that will encapsulate what Frank Kelly has meant in my life. He has guided me back to God. He has emulated the St. Francis Xavier goal of "Salvation of All Souls". I trust him implicitly with anything in my life because he is a righteous man.

Most importantly, he has taught me the value of prayer and that it does work on my life. I still get anxious, but know where to go with the feeling. Sometimes Frank and I laugh about how he heard the message from God that night at Fr. McDonough's Mass about someone coming in and going out. I don't know if I would have come back. Thanks to Frank and many others, I continue to practice my faith and pray that I grow in my conviction of God's Love on a daily basis.

I am only one of many that Frank continues to help. He and his family are in my prayer intentions each day, and I know that my family is in his prayers. I couldn't have a better friend.

(Joseph McCusker)

Wisdom and Strength through Catholic Socrates

I am deeply indebted to Frank Kelly, mainly because he interceded to the good for a family member who was experiencing a major spiritual crisis. Frank knew true things that had previously occurred and that I had never related to him. People involved in precipitating this spiritual crisis somehow also entered Frank's life -- seemingly coincidentally without human explanation. It seems that the situation will resolve itself on account of these factors. Frank had a deep impact there.

As far as I am concerned, I have sometimes felt a need to talk with Frank, and then a few minutes later the phone would ring and it would be him. He knows things about me that I don't tell him. He knows what I am thinking without having to relate it to him. He always reminds me of what I already know. I compare him to a Catholic Socrates.

In August 2001 my father (who was eighty-two years old) was seriously injured in a car accident in the driveway. My sister called Frank without my knowledge. After Frank arrived at the hospital and prayed over my father, he said that my father was at peace. When I came home, I cried myself to sleep, thinking he was going to die. Then he seemed to make a miraculous recovery after five days in intensive care, with his broken arm in the process of healing. But after coming home, he started not to look well. I again started to cry, thinking he was going to die. Again I cried myself to sleep. I made an appointment to have his cast changed. The doctor told me to take him to the emergency room. But when I drove home to my parents' house, he was dying in my mother's arms. I called 9-1-1 and an ambulance came and took him to the hospital. But he died on the way.

Someone called Frank before the funeral and Frank suggested that the priest do three particular readings. These accurately captured my father's character and life. It was uncanny. I thought in church that I couldn't have done a better job myself in choosing these readings. But Frank didn't even know my father (other than from the one encounter in the hospital room). It's as though he saw my father's soul when he prayed over my father.

I had the impression that Frank had foreseen what was going to happen -- giving me peace of mind about my father and the courage to accept his death. There is a holy strength and a loving nonjudgmentalness about Frank that most people don't seem to have. Because of him, my faith is stronger and I get a certain peace that things are always okay no matter what happens. I think he is an angel with human flaws.

(Joan Danko)

Peace through Deep Faith and Knowledge

Peace in the stressful times of the twentieth and twenty-first centuries is difficult to find. Frank Kelly has this peace through his faith. He knows individuals beyond the surface. He can call up an appropriate Bible passage without an individual specifying a problem. The mystery remains "how". Why is he concerned with people whom he does not know? He gives of his time freely without reward or expectation.

He has shared his gift of prayer with me over the last several years. The most special time was on the evening of August 11, 2001. As I was leaving the house to bring my son to the emergency room, my uncle was at the foot of the stairs with my mother: "Your father was taken by ambulance to the hospital, he was in an accident."

While we were waiting in the ER, I called Frank and he was home. He said a prayer that made me feel that my father would okay. In the ER a surgeon was stitching his left arm; he needed in excess of one hundred stitches. The airbag in the car had caused contusions to his heart and lungs and broken his ribs and fingers, perhaps from his eyeglasses. The impact caused his body to react as a heart attack. As difficult as it was, after we spent a few minutes with him, I took my mother home to get rest for his recovery. He had the time in CCU and a few difficult days. Frank came to Worcester to pray over him in CCU. The hospital priest gave him the final blessings (last rites). The twenty-four hour monitoring continued. On Thursday he was sent home. He was improving but had trouble with his digestion.

My son Vaughn started school the next week. Grandpa always walked Vaughn to the bus stop, made sure he had breakfast, and gave him extra money for ice cream. On Vaughn's first day of school, he cheerfully came at 6 AM to wake Vaughn, get him breakfast, and make sure he was ready for school. This will always be a special memory, as we never thought he would come home from the hospital.

My father died on August 27. Frank picked out the readings for the funeral and attended the Mass. He's been supportive to my sister, mother, and myself by his calls and prayers. What he knows and does must have a vision beyond the norm.

(Frances Slowaski)

Ripple Effects of Peace and Good

My personal experience with Frank Kelly began in the Spring of 1997. Frank was conducting a Life in the Spirit seminar in February, 1997. I had never heard of Frank. A friend, Jim, had met me in 1994 or 1995 at my local parish. Jim was a scholar with an encyclopedic knowledge of many details of Catholic Church history and theology. I chanced to call him, and, since he was preparing for the priesthood, I asked him what made him so certain that he had a vocation to the priesthood. Jim cited some experiences from his life that appeared to confirm his vocation. Among these experiences he described an encounter with Frank Kelly. I showed some surprise at the experiences, which appeared to be highly unusual chance meetings with Frank. Jim gave me Frank's phone number and invited me to call Frank if I doubted any of Jim's story. I called Frank as soon as I hung up the phone from my call with Jim. Frank invited me to attend the Life in the Spirit seminar.

Jim and I drove out to St. Brendan's in Bellingham the next

evening. There was a severe ice storm as we approached Rte. 495. Nonetheless, we arrived safely and heard Rosaleen's testimony. It was beautiful. I was very moved, and as we all prepared to go home, Frank prayed over each person who desired prayer. That prayer was the beginning of greater peace. I was in the midst of losing my house through foreclosure and bankruptcy. I should have been in total anxiety, but I was not. I was peaceful. As my own life became more and more peaceful, I sent people to Frank when they needed peace. As a lawyer, my days are filled with people in trouble of one sort or another. Even in speaking with my family members, I would send those looking for peace to Frank Kelly. After five years the network of people touched by Frank is enormous. My two youngest brothers have both prayed with Frank many times and experienced deep conversions in their lives. They too have enjoyed great peace in their prayer with Frank. Clients with troubled histories or mental illness have found the same peace and conversion.

Of all the things that I have observed in dealing with Frank, I am most surprised by and impressed with the way God has used Frank to touch many people in a sort of network. It is not unusual to see Frank touch one person, who in turn touches another -- until there is a linkage of five or more people. The "good" done is enormously multiplied.

The fruits of these contacts are increased peace, conversion of life, deepened regular prayer, and good example set for even more people.

(Dave Culliton, Atty.)

Cure of Carpal Tunnel Syndrome

I longed in my heart first to have "everything" fixed. In time I longed only for peace. Later I longed for the Gifts of the Spirit. Frank talked to me most weeks and sent more witness tapes. My brother Dave who was also praying with Frank talked to me too. My brother encouraged me to keep praying also.

After my brother had sent me a "Life in the Spirit" booklet and Frank had sent several more tapes, Frank told me has was coming to Erie, PA, to do a "Life in the Spirit" retreat with Rosaleen at her parish. Erie was only one-hundred miles from Buffalo, so I concocted a story for the home front and hoped a friend would come with me. Two people I had asked said they couldn't make it. About two weeks before I was to go, a nurse came to my office as a patient. We had talked before about Our Lady. I shared with her my prayer experiences with Frank. She had previously done a Life in the Spirit Seminar. She wanted to meet Frank. She said she would go to Erie with me. I had an old bright red sports car that I drove to Erie. I wasn't sure why I was going, but I went. We went first to Rosaleen's house, where we met Frank. I think he asked, when he met me at the curb, "How was the drive?" I told him I wasn't sure why I was there.

For about six months I had been suffering with a severe carpal tunnel syndrome in my right wrist. The use of it hurt in my podiatric work each day and especially at surgery. It stung a lot and I couldn't really put a lot of pressure on with my grip. We arrived at the church with Frank and a prayer service began. Frank took the nurse and me to a back chapel. He asked us if we wanted to be prayed over. I guess we both said "sure". I sat down. He put his hands on my head and asked me if there were any physical problems. I mentioned my wrist. He prayed over me. I didn't know what to think. I felt like I was half-asleep and half-awake. I think my head was bowed down. I could see Frank backing away from me saying, "Just leave him alone for awhile" and something about "slain in the spirit". When I got up a few minutes later, he came over to me and asked how I was. During the period just afterward, I could see him praying over the nurse. My wrist pain seemed much better. Over the next few weeks it disappeared. In severe exertion I feel a weakness but no pain.

I could feel God's loving touch. I started to read and pray more. I went to Mass whenever I could. At least two or three times a month I prayed with Frank. I started to think about confession more. Frank encouraged me to pick a regular confessor. I met a Byzantine rite priest by the name of Fr. Joseph Bertha. He introduced me to many subjects to study. He also became my confessor. I started going to Saturday Mass. He would hear my confession right after Mass.

I had had problems with my anger for my whole life. One of my brothers had given up alcohol and seemed much more peaceful. In prayer with Frank I thought my spousal anger would improve with no alcohol. It seems to work. Frank often tells me after it's over that he has fasted forty days for my wife and children and our intentions. I started trying to fast on Wednesday and do a partial fast with full abstinence on Friday. This past Easter my wife started to go to daily Mass.

In my work I do some foot surgery. When the results are best it seems like *I* was having a bad day. One day I looked at a foot I was almost finished with, but then realized another toe needed correction. I did it; however, I had not anesthetized that part of the foot. The patient never felt it and had a good result. Thank you, God.

My wrist pain never returned like it had been. Many times I hope to go to Mass on First Fridays and all of a sudden a surgery will be delayed or canceled and I can go. Praise the Lord.

Thank you, Frank. Praise be to Jesus.

(Dr. Phil Culliton)

Emma's Story and a Word of Knowledge

My wife Polly and I were delighted by the news that she was pregnant. A routine ultrasound performed early in the course of her pregnancy revealed a low lying placenta. We were not particularly concerned about this finding, since we read that it is common early in pregnancy. While she was in her third trimester, her obstetrician ordered a special "high risk" ultrasound, because my wife was thirty-seven years old. This was performed in early July, 2001. It is here that the story really begins.

I left work in the late morning in order to meet Polly at the hospital for the ultrasound test. As the technician performed the exam, she informed us that my wife's amniotic fluid level was low. She asked Polly whether she had experienced any leakage of fluid. She then called in a particular hospital's maternal-fetal medicine specialist. It was then that we experienced one of the great shocks of our lives and certainly the most disappointing news of my wife's pregnancy. The physician informed us that the amniotic fluid level was critically low and that Polly had likely suffered a leak of amniotic fluid. He told us that the baby was at great risk and could die from either infection or from the umbilical cord being impinged (in which case the baby's supply of oxygen and nutrients could be cut off). He advised that my wife be induced into labor that day. This would mean having a baby that was about five weeks premature and therefore a stay in the intensive care nursery.

We decided to see Polly's obstetrician Dr. Intengen. He performed a test and found no evidence of leakage of amniotic fluid. He added that the placenta was overlying her old C-section

92

scar and that a potential complication known as *placenta accreta* could occur, possibly requiring an emergency hysterectomy. He advised us to seek a second opinion from the group of maternal-fetal medicine specialists at our local children's hospital. After we arrived at the hospital, Polly was placed on a fetal monitor to check the baby's heart-rate. In the meantime I called Polly's mother, who reminded me of a highly regarded physician by the name of Dr. Bruce Rodgers, a member of the children's hospital maternal-fetal medicine department. As it was late in the afternoon, we would receive as a consultant whoever was on call that evening. Within a relatively short period of time, Dr. Bruce Rodgers walked through the door, and soon our hope of having a healthy, full-term baby would be restored. I believe to this day that Dr. Rodgers was heaven-sent.

Dr. Rodgers' calm, reassuring manner helped to quell our fears and lift our spirits. He asked us a long list of questions. He seemed to sense our fear and anxiety, and with a gentle smile led us away from the troubling emotions. He then performed a long thorough ultrasound, concluding that multiple pockets of fluid were present and the baby's situation was not in fact critical. He advised that we may well be able to really go full-term, but that it may be necessary to perform weekly ultrasounds and "non-stress" tests to monitor the baby's condition and the level of the amniotic fluid. He further advised that Polly drink fluid (I believe about one liter per day) to encourage improvement in the amniotic fluid level. He added, of course, that if Polly noticed any decrease in the baby's movement, she should report it immediately to either himself or Dr. Intengen.

The next five weeks were far from pleasant. Each evening we would nervously fall asleep hoping that Polly would not notice any decreased movement on the part of the baby. The ultrasounds and "non-stress" tests were pure torture, as we would await conclusions regarding amniotic fluid levels, which would go up and down. The nurse would reposition the monitor head, as we would experience brief periods in which we would no longer hear the baby's heart, only to be shortly reassured that this was a false alarm simply due to head "placement".

I attended Mass each day, mostly at St. Gregory the Great church, praying for Polly and the baby's well-being. For some reason after Mass one day, I struck up a conversation with Dr. Phil Culliton, a member of the parish. A very kind and good man, Dr. Culliton assured me of his prayers. In addition, he advised that I call a guy by the name of Frank Kelly. I kept Mr. Kelly's number but did not call him right away, thinking it a bit strange to call someone in Boston whom I had never met. Within a short period of time, I again saw Dr. Culliton at Mass. He told me: "Frank said the baby will be fine." I of course was happy to hear any reassuring news, but was uncertain of what to make of it. I finally decided to call Frank Kelly.

My first conversation with Frank Kelly was a long one lasting about one hour. Frank advised that I pray to St. Gerard Majella, the patron saint of pregnant women, as well as to St. Elizabeth, the patron saint of mothers. He again assured me not to worry, that the baby would be well. Frank prayed "angelically" -- my first introduction to such prayer. He gave me a Psalm to read, which he always does at the close of our conversations. He then asked me whether I felt peace, which he has continuously reminded me is God's great desire for us. He assured me of his continued prayers for Polly and the baby.

Over the course of the next few weeks I continued to attend Mass on a regular basis and pray the Rosary. I went to our local Carmelite monastery and wrote a note to the sisters describing our situation and asking for their prayers. They responded with a personal hand-written note assuring us of their prayers, a prayer card, and an Agnus Dei necklace. I also called my relatives in Ireland -- Tom and Frankie Harte. Frankie told me she would immediately go to the Carmelite monastery in Knock, Ireland, and ask for their prayers for my wife and our baby. My father attended Mass and made a novena to Our Lady of Guadalupe in addition to his daily Rosary. I asked various priests in our area for their prayers. I also requested the prayers of a wonderful holy woman (Margie Richards), who works at our local Jesuit church, St. Michael's. Last, but not least, we had all the members of my wife's family, as well as my six brothers and sisters, praying on a regular basis that all would go well.

We had hoped for a natural childbirth, but as Polly's due date became closer, the prospects of this happening diminished. Late ultrasounds continued to show the presence of a low lying placenta. An ultrasound done just a week prior to what turned out to be Emma's date of birth showed that the umbilical cord was wrapped once around the baby's neck. Just a few days prior to Polly's due date, an ultrasound again showed the presence of a low lying placenta over the site of her old C-section scar. I consulted an obstetrician friend of mine, asking him whether there was any possibility of the placenta moving to a higher, more normal position this late in the pregnancy. He responded that there was not. He added that, given the situation, we should sign a consent so that (if need be) a hysterectomy could be performed, since the risk of placenta accreta was present. Needless to say, I was not happy with his assessment.

On Thursday, August 16, 2001, we met with Polly's obstetrician Dr. Intengen. Given all of the above circumstances and his exam that day, he advised that it would be unlikely that Polly would go into natural childbirth any time soon and that it made most sense to proceed with a C-section. Polly agreed, so we made plans to prepare for a C-section the following morning.

We arrived at the children's hospital early on the morning of Friday, August 17. Polly was hooked up to the monitor in the labor and delivery wing as we waited for her to be called to the O.R.

From start to finish the nurses and physicians who served us that day were kind, gentle, and outstanding in the application of their professional skills. Polly asked to wear the Agnus Dei necklace. Both while in our room and in the O.R., I constantly prayed the Rosary and would frequently touch the crucifix to Polly. When the anesthesiologist gave the signal, Dr. Intengen began his work. Within a short period of time, we heard the cry of a big (8 lb., 5 oz.), beautiful baby girl. In addition to this wonderful news, just prior to Emma Mary's arrival I was overjoyed to hear Dr. Intengen state that the placenta was "out of the way". In other words, during the course of the final 2-3 days of my wife's pregnancy, the placenta had in fact moved up and away from my wife's old C-section scar. The terrible possibility of *placenta accreta* and a hysterectomy had miraculously disappeared.

Ten months later, Emma Mary is a beautiful healthy baby girl. She is crawling and climbing and spends a good part of her day laughing and smiling with her big brother and sister. She is a true joy in our lives and we are tremendously grateful to God for her. In addition we are very grateful to all our family members and friends whose prayers we know were greatly instrumental in bringing about the birth of our healthy baby.

(Dr. Paul Hart)

Physical Healings and Employment

I have had a number of experiences with Frank Kelly that you may have an interest in learning about.

Since I have known Frank, I have suffered from serious back pain and also had a painful bout with what was something like Carpal Tunnel Syndrome/RSI Repetitive Stress Syndrome in both hands. I have to say I was freaking out about both the hands and back conditions (I did get a cortisone shot in one of the hands). Frank had prayed over me a number of times about both conditions, and would tell me that it would go away after a certain period of time. Often, I was in disbelief. When I have been in such pain over a long period of time, I have been challenged -- physically, mentally, and spiritually. I started losing hope that things would get any better. I felt like a disaster. I am happy to say that I no longer have pain in my back or my hands. Thank God.

I have also made a difficult job change that Frank had helped with significantly. He has given me a couple of very specific words of knowledge during this very difficult transition. When I was still a stockbroker I was seriously considering graduate school of some kind. Many of the programs I looked at were on average two years. During this period of time Frank prayed about it and said I would be going to school, but not as long as two years. It turned out that I went to a computer technical school for just over a year.

Additionally, after I had found my first job in the computer industry, where I was employed for five months, I started to look for another job. Frank prayed about this and mentioned that someone by the name of "Tom" would be helping me get my new job. After sending my résumé to forty companies and having one interview, my father sent my résumé to a friend of his named Tom. My résumé was then given to his son-in-law, who helped me get a new position where I am presently.

Thank God.

(Chris Clark)

Healing of Back Injury

I first met Frank Kelly during the Jubilee year at a Life in the Spirit seminar he was giving. I was fascinated by his testimony and quite moved by his strong faith. When he spoke, Scripture came alive. I heard how Frank's life had been changed by God and I observed how he lived.

Six months after I met Frank, I sustained a painful back injury. He prayed over me and believed Jesus would heal me. I often felt I would not be healed, but Frank encouraged me to pray and trust. I began to recover. During this experience I learned about suffering and how to benefit from it. I witnessed Frank's example. I learned that uniting any pain or difficulty in life to Jesus' suffering affords a wonderful opportunity for grace and growth.

Frank gives unselfishly of his time and energy, with no thought of personal reward. He practices what he preaches. It is very clear to me that the Holy Spirit is moving mightily through Frank.

(Kathleen L. Clark)

Clarifications through Words of Knowledge

In 1992 a woman I knew who attended a prayer group was prayed over by Frank Kelly. He asked her if she knew a "Tim". She answered "yes", and Frank said: "Pray for him, be open with him, and give him time." She told me this after my return from a world-wide back-pack trip, during which I met a man who had a great deal of interest in some mind-boggling ideas that included end-times prophecies. I told her that I would like to go to that prayer group and meet Frank. I went to the prayer group with a big manila envelope containing a lot of literature about end-times prophecies. When the prayer meeting was over, Frank invited me to his apartment. I was sitting at his kitchen table, but he was standing at the sink with his back turned to me. I mentioned that I had something to show him, and he shot back: "I suppose you're going to tell me the Pope is the Antichrist." I was flabbergasted, because he couldn't possibly have seen through the thick manila envelope with the literature inside.

I continued going to the prayer group to relearn my Faith. Frank explained a lot of things to me that I never understood.

As far as some other specific words of knowledge go, in 1994 or 1995 there was a pile of lumber sitting on a friend's lawn. I was asked to get rid of it with my truck. I should have refused, but instead I beat around the bush and finally offered to take the wood away, even though I didn't really want to do it. I delayed in carrying out this favor. Later, when I was pressed to remove the wood, I tried to make excuses to avoid the bother. The person became very upset. I called Frank for a prayer, and he got Proverbs 6:1-5, which speaks about being trapped in promises and how to get released from the commitment. I flipped through the book of Proverbs, and found that this was the only passage that pertained to my situation!

Over the years Frank has given me many Scripture verses that were right on the money. For example, a couple of times when I was confused about some points and asked him to pray with me, he got 1 Timothy 1:5-7 and 2 Timothy 4:3-5, both of which warn about false teachings. I knew these readings were right on the money.

(Tim Ramey)

Knocked Out by the Holy Spirit

In order to understand what happened between Frank Kelly and me, it would help to know where I was in January, 1997.

I wouldn't let "any" healing type pray over me, nor any

"laying of hands". Jesus Christ wasn't part of my life; it was God the Father and I.

In March, 1997, my wife and I were going to Rome for an audience with the Pope. But one of my knees was the size of a basketball. I knew Frank but had never let him pray over me. I was in so much pain that I let him pray and lay hands on me. When he was finished, my knee was a normal size, and the pain was gone.

In May, 1997, while at a prayer meeting I was having severe chest pain. No one in the room knew of my discomfort. Frank came across the room, put his hand on my chest, and started praying. When he was finished, he said it was not my heart; it was a little asthma, which has been diagnosed since then.

In late June, 1997, Frank said that the Holy Spirit was coming to visit me -- to which I responded: "What does He want for dinner?" Mr. Kelly told me to pray through the intercession of the Immaculate Heart of Mary, to let Jesus into my heart.

In September, 1997, while on a pilgrimage, a priest from England prayed over me and said the exact words that Frank had said in June. That very night I was praying to let Jesus into my heart through the intercession of the Immaculate Heart of Mary. Something came out of the sun and knocked me out. When I came to, Frank was standing near me, saying: "I told you HE was coming to see you."

In June, 1998, my brother was dying. I asked Frank to say a prayer for him. After he finished saying his prayers, he told me not to worry; even though my brother was in a coma, Frank knew that the priest was giving him the last rites.

During the time of my brother's coma, the last rites *were* given to him just before he died.

(Hugh Treanor)

Aura and Relief from Worry

When Frank Kelly was speaking, it was as if God was whispering in his ear. I was just so touched by every word he said. My heart felt like it was on fire!

As I was intently watching and listening to him, I started to notice an aura around him. I looked away a few times, but each time I looked back at him the aura was there! I asked one of my friends if she noticed anything around Frank's head, and she looked at me a little strange. We took our lunch bread, and I asked another friend of mine, and she said that she too noticed it, but did not want to say anything. When Frank resumed his afternoon talk, the aura was stronger than ever, and I noticed what seemed to be shadows or dark outlines of three bodies behind Frank entwined with this aura. I presumed they were saints or even Padre Pio, as Frank has such a strong devotion. I was completely overcome with this experience and thankful for it.

Also, when Frank prayed over me, he told me I have been praying very hard for my children and especially my son. He revealed to me that my son would be okay and to let go of the burden I was carrying around with me. I was stunned, as this was so true. My son was going through some very difficult times in his life. And I was so very troubled and worried by it that it was consuming a lot of my mental energy.

Also, Frank told me to stop looking for another job, as God wants me where I am right now. You see, I am the Religious Director at our parish, and have been seriously considering leaving next year (no one knew of my plans). I felt that there wasn't much more I could do for our parish. I guess now God has other plans for me.

Meeting Frank has changed my outlook on life. He is truly a spirited and blessed person chosen by our Lord to spread the love of God.

(Sheryl Skowronski)

Aura, Knowledge, and Wisdom

Before our Life in the Spirit seminar, Frank Kelly told me that I had been praying for the gift of knowledge; this was indeed a fact. Later, when praying with me, he told me that where my health was concerned, I would be victorious. (I have cancer.) Frank also told me that I had also been praying for the gift of wisdom, which was also true, and that I would see fruits from this seminar. (That was so important to me, since my heart has been burdened for several years about an outpouring of the Holy Spirit in our parish.)

While Frank was giving his Saturday talks, I was amazed to see an aura around his body; my friend Sheryl had also witnessed this. Our group was touched by Frank's simplicity and by his humble nature. In sharing with others who had attended the seminar, I found out that many were shocked over Frank's knowledge about events in their lives; they felt so blessed to have had this experience.

(Luvinia LaDuke)

Words for Mind and Body

Some years ago, before my appointment with a psychologist, Frank Kelly prayed over the phone and gave me Psalm 139. After my arrival at the psychologist's office, during the course of our talk he mentioned Psalm 139. I was stunned.

A few years later when I was feeling very sick, I asked

Frank to pray with me over the phone. He told me to go to the hospital because I had pneumonia. I went to a clinic, but they told me my sickness was not pneumonia. Since they didn't know what it was, I then went to a different medical center. There the doctor diagnosed pneumonia. So Frank had known more through his word of knowledge than the health professionals at the first clinic knew. I was amazed.

About a year after that I was seriously considering furthering my education. But I thought it might be too late in the school year to take an exam for entering graduate school the following Fall, yet Frank told me to take the exam anyway. (He even offered to pay the fee for me to take it!) He said that St. Thomas Aquinas would help me and that I would get into a good graduate school. It turns out that I did very well on the exam and *was* accepted into graduate school (even receiving a favorable early decision). Although Frank had predicted some of this, he also said beforehand and afterwards that it was all God's doing.

(Name Withheld)

Words Get to the Heart

I met Frank Kelly in 2001 at a "Life in the Spirit" seminar he led at St. Brendan Catholic Church in Bellingham, Massachusetts. In the church hall after Mass that evening, I was surprised to see how people crowded around him. He prayed over each person, conveyed a message of healing, and recommended a passage from Scripture to reflect upon.

As I found out, Frank is a kind, gracious, and welcoming person who is quick to point out the sacrifices and achievements of others, but never his own. He is extremely generous with his time and his prayers. One immediately feels comfortable in his presence.

He shares jokes and amusing stories with ease. He is usually smiling, despite the physical ailments that he endures. A calm, relaxed quality in his own life extends to those around him.

Frank listens intently. His ability to discern what's really going on in someone's life is sometimes temporarily masked by a rambling quality in his stories. While the stories seem to be culled from ordinary moments in life, one later realizes that Frank's words get to the heart of God's message.

Frank brings a quiet reverence for God to his work. "Praise God" is frequently heard in his conversations. He prays with a confident, hopeful spirit. I am certain that his prayers and gentle guidance bring spiritual peace, healing, and comfort to all who ask him to pray for them or their loved ones. His is a positive voice of the Father's love.

(Diane Burak)

Correct Physical and Spiritual Diagnosis

I have known Frank Kelly for many years. He has told me many little things that turned out to be correct.

But the one biggest thing concerns Phil, the son of a friend of mine. Many times Phil was dying in intensive care in the hospital, suffering from cirrhosis of the liver. The doctors would give him twenty-four hours to live on account of his five percent liver function accompanied by bleeding. Frank went a couple of times to two different hospitals where Phil was staying, and there prayed over Phil. Once Frank told Phil that God would heal him if he would turn to Him. Another time Frank prayed with Phil when he was unconscious, yet tears were coming into his eyes. When I asked Frank why Phil was crying, he replied that God was revealing his sinfulness to him. Yet another time when Phil was in the hospital, Frank prayed with me for him, and said that Phil was going to get arrested and go to jail. His mother and I thought Frank was crazy, because Phil was dying. Within two weeks Phil had recovered, was arrested, and went to jail. Frank also told me at least three times that Phil was sick and would again land in the hospital, and, sure enough, each time he did.

Phil once told his mother that during one of his operations he saw angels around him, and when he saw this vision he knew that he was going to make it, because God was working to take care of him again. Remarkably, Frank had told me prior to this incident that God would reveal something to Phil.

So many times Frank told me when praying about Phil that God would heal him if he would turn to God. A number of times when Frank prayed with me about Phil, Frank got Scripture readings about evil and corruption, which his mother and I knew had to do with the way Phil was living (basically related to drug abuse). One time when Phil had been in prison for almost a year, just before he got out, the doctor said that his liver had improved a great deal. It's a miracle that someone could have even survived with so little liver function. Once Phil had to have seven pints of transfused blood (I believe the body holds only around eight pints), and Frank accurately predicted that Phil would be okay, even though the doctors said he was going to die. Frank has been right every time about Phil whenever any crisis occurred. Frank told us many years ago that Phil's recovery would be a long, hard road. He was right, because Phil still hasn't come around. Frank thinks that Phil will eventually go to confession and reform his life, and will then experience a complete healing. I feel that Masses and prayers have been helping to keep him alive up to now.

I have been working in prison ministry for many years. Frank would pray over some of the men in prison and tell them personal things (such as about family members). They would then ask me whether I had talked about them to Frank, but I never had.

They couldn't understand how Frank knew these things without being told in advance about them. They would ask Frank how he knew about these things, and Frank would respond that *he* didn't know but that God knew and had told him.

(Betty Slaney)

Conditional Healing of Angina

I had been volunteering at the local soup kitchen for about three years and had known Frank Kelly for about five years, when one of the other volunteers asked me what a Life in the Spirit seminar was and who did them in the area. After explaining about the seminar and some of the gifts of the Holy Spirit, I told him it's done for 1-2 hours per week for seven weeks and sometimes over the course of a whole week-end. He was interested in going through one, but there weren't any in the area at the time. When I later told this to Frank, he suggested using the audio tapes of a recent seminar he had given. After further discussing this option with people at the soup kitchen, we decided to hold it for seven straight weeks at the home of one of the volunteers right after the soup kitchen closed down at 7 PM. It was only a small group, a few of the volunteers and a few people who came to the soup kitchen on a regular basis.

One week after another went by, until it was the fifth week of the seminar. The theme for the fifth week is "Baptism in the Holy Spirit". On this week, instead of the normal structure of prayer, singing, witnessing, etc., a Mass is usually said and one or more people with various gifts of the Holy Spirit pray over people while laying hands on them. This serves as a "rekindling" of the Holy Spirit, which the person already received during the Sacrament of Baptism and then more powerfully during the Sacrament of Confirmation, if the person is Catholic. Because this week is sort of the high point of the seminar and because Fr. Tacelli would be coming a good distance from Boston with Frank to say the Mass and pray over people, Frank suggested we invite more people to the Mass, even though they weren't going through the whole seminar.

One of the people who came from the soup kitchen just for the fifth week was a man in his 50's who was a lukewarm Catholic. (We'll call him John.) John was a practicing homosexual who rarely went to Mass. Sometimes is was for legitimate health reasons, but he agreed that if he just made a little more effort, he could go most of the time. His real problem was that he didn't want to accept the Church's teaching on his lifestyle and opted to stay home on Sundays, just reading the Bible.

So, on the night of the "baptism", Fr. Tacelli offered to hear confession for anyone who wanted to go. During this time Frank was giving his witness to the group. Much to my surprise, John sprang up and went to confession. When he came out, he said: "Boy, did he straighten me right out! He straightened me out like a toothpick. He doesn't fool around." After Frank's witnessing and confessions were over (most people went to confession -- about fifteen), we had the Mass and John received Holy Communion under both species.

After Mass, Fr. Tacelli blessed people with holy oil while Frank prayed over them. John was one of the last to get prayed over. I heard John start to breathe really deeply and start moaning. When I looked around, Fr. Tacelli was right next to him with the holy oil and Frank was praying over John with his hand on his chest. John's knees were buckling and Frank was half-holding him up with his other hand. Frank motioned to me to catch him, because with his arthritis he wouldn't have been able to hold John. John's moans started getting louder and more intense. He seemed like he might pass out, so we sat him down in a chair. After awhile, it subsided and John relaxed. Everyone was mingling and having refreshments.

Before we left, I asked John about what had happened. He informed me that he had angina in his chest and always needed an inhaler to help him breathe. He said: "When Frank prayed over me and put his hand on my chest, it felt like Jesus was opening up my chest. I thought I was dying. I can breathe a lot better now."

A couple of weeks later, when I saw him at the soup kitchen, I asked John how his breathing was. He said he used to need his inhaler just to go up a flight of stairs, but he had hardly used it since Frank prayed over him during the "baptism". Then he praised God.

A few more weeks went by, but the next time I saw him he looked worse than I had ever seen him. He even needed help walking around from a friend of his and was using the inhaler constantly. After speaking with his friend, who told me John had been an excellent athlete all his life, I learned that he had continued to be obstinate in his homosexual lifestyle and was refusing to go to Mass on Sundays. After being cleansed during confession with Fr. Tacelli and receiving grace from God, who had mercy on him and his health problem, he would not change his ways and didn't want to hear about it from anyone. When I called Frank and asked him about this, he said that, because John remained in his sin without repentance, the angina came back worse than ever.

(Michael Judge)

A Word for Generosity

About nine years ago, I was writing a book on the effects of abortion. Many publishers thought it had merit, but did not want to publish it. Finally, I obtained a publisher, but he required $3,000 to print the book. I told a friend about this situation, who then mentioned it to another friend, who thereupon told Frank Kelly (I did not know Frank at the time). Frank, when told about the problem, asked why can't the book get published. He was told that $3,000 was required to print the book and the author (myself) was out of work and did not have the funds. Frank prayed about it and was told by God to put up the money for the book. Frank contacted his friend and passed the money and prayer along to me thereby allowing the book to get published. Upon hearing the good news, I contacted Frank directly and that began a long period of getting to know this man who walks by faith.

At times, I have spoken to Frank and it is clear that he has the gifts of the Holy Spirit. I spoke to him on the day that I lost a job and he immediately revealed that it was a job loss that was not due to my fault, but rather due to supervisory jealousy. Over the years, Frank has impressed me with his perseverance to spread the truths of Catholicism as well as introduce others to the Holy Spirit.

I have been further impressed with this man, who, despite his sufferings and difficulties, has not given up his smile, nor ever fails to shine the light of Christ onto all he meets. Frank patiently listens, prays, and shines the light of Christ onto anyone that God brings onto his path in life.

(Lawrence F. Roberge)

[Note from the Editor: Prof. Roberge's book *The Cost of Abortion* is available from Life Cycle Books, LPO Box 1008, Niagara Falls, NY 14304-1008, Tel. (800)214-5849. It is very informative and highly recommended for explaining our contemporary socio-economic plight.]

Words for Friends

I met Frank five years ago and was initially struck by his down-to-earth personality. My husband (at the time, beau) had told me a little about Frank and what to expect when I met him. We picked up Frank in Stockbridge, Mass., at the National Shrine of the Divine Mercy. As he gave us a tour of the chapel, I sensed the Holy Spirit was with us every step of the way.

At our second meeting (six months or so later), Lawrence and I took Frank out for lunch. The lunch was uneventful and then we dropped Frank off at his apartment. He turned and said to me: "You know those two boys (students) you are concerned about, try not to worry." Frank then told me a passage to read from the Bible. After Frank left, I spoke to my husband and said that I had not ever mentioned those two students to Frank. I then realized that Frank has the Holy Spirit working through him. Every time I have spoken with Frank, I am more aware of the presence of the Holy Spirit.

Recently we visited Frank for a week and were fortunate to stay at his home. Frank would calm worries that I had about friends and a job situation (at the time, I was interviewing for a new job). One of the evenings, I was asking Frank to pray for friends' premature baby. Frank replied: "The baby will be fine. However, the problem is that your friend is having problems with her son. Tell her to pray to (unknown saint)". Again, I was in awe of Frank, since I had not mentioned that my friend was having problems with her son. Frank is a true vessel for the Holy Spirit to perform works of God.

(Cynthia Roberge)

Someone with Special Spiritual Powers

I had just returned from Ghana in September of 1998, after half a year's research work on my doctoral thesis, when a lady whom I had never met before introduced herself to me as Ms. Patricia

Conners. This was after a noonday's Mass at St. Mary's Catholic Church in Randolph, Mass. It was through the instrumentality of her that I got to know Mr. Francis Kelly (popularly called "Frank Kelly").

Long before I finally met him in his house still under construction in Marshfield, Mass., Pat had told me a great deal about him. She had made me to understand that Frank is a prayerful man, who prays not only for himself but also for anyone who needs his prayers and for the universal Church. She convinced me that Frank has some special spiritual powers, which include healing and seeing the future. Accordingly, Frank had told her during one of their conversations that she would soon have to go to the hospital for a procedure. She would suffer tremendously as a result of that procedure, but eventually she would be okay. According to Pat, true to Frank's words, she went to the hospital for surgery. Unfortunately, she was given an overdose of anesthesia. The consequences were horrendous, just as Frank had predicted or prophesied.

After all these stories, I was jazzed up to meet Frank. The opportunity finally came when Pat offered to drive me to Marshfield. It seemed like I knew him even before we finally met. He too must have heard a lot about me from Pat, for our first meeting was very informal. I was conducted around his house. I chose one of the bedrooms as my future room. We found ourselves outside the house and he offered to pray with me. Whoever refuses a prayer? So I consented, and Pat (who was with us) politely walked back into the house. We were now alone. He placed his hands over my head and prayed in the English language for about two minutes. After that, the prayer turned into a chant in a language unknown to me. It was none of the major European or African languages. At the end of it all, he passed a judgment: "You are a perfectionist." This took me by surprise, because that is precisely what I am. I was wondering how he could come to this conclusion after such a short encounter. Could "flesh and blood" have revealed this to him? I also passed a judgment, though a guarded one: "This man is either a very good psychologist or a seer."

There are many remarkable things about Frank. He is one of the few people I have met who after praying for you gives you a Scriptural text to read in addition. Sometimes the relevance of the text to what you are praying for is apparent and sometimes one has to reflect to see the relevance.

Frank is still a man of faith in spite of the many misfortunes in his life on account of his faith. To see Frank is to see a man who has endured sufferings. Yet he does not complain as the prophet Jeremiah, or at least I have not heard him complain.

I had the privilege to have been invited to one of Frank's healing services at St. Brendan's Church in Bellingham, Mass. The service was preceded by a concelebrated Mass presided over by Rev. Ronald Tacelli, S.J. After the Mass Frank shared his faith experience with the participants. The healing service commenced with two priests, Fr. John Peters and myself, anointing the participants who then went to Frank for healing prayer. As he prayed over them, to my amazement some of the people appeared to be losing consciousness, became rigid, started falling backward, and had to be supported gently and calmly to the floor. I had heard of such a thing happening only in "spiritual" [Pentecostal, ed.] churches, whose detractors claim the pastors deliberately push their victims down while attributing their falling to the reception of the Spirit. At first, I thought he was using the "spiritual" churches' tactics. Consequently, I observed critically. I noticed that Frank never touched the heads of those he was praying for. In most cases, there was at least half an inch or one inch of space between Frank's hands and the head of the one he was praying over. Yet they fell. Were they overwhelmed by the presence of the Holy Spirit? When it was my turn, I was thinking of how I would fall, if

I were to fall. But the prayer ended and I was still on my feet.

(Fr. Peter Ayirago, Ph.D.)

The Prophet Who Was a Bit Much

Come and See

"Come and See," Mary smiled. "They're a nice group of people; you'll like them. We are starting with a pot luck dinner, then hymns and readings and prayers and ... *special* things happen. Do come." My beautiful Mary, speaking words of love, pleading with her tear-filled eyes, "Do Come."

I hesitated, hating to disappoint my best friend of fourteen years. I was hurting, sick and heart-broken, really in no mood to socialize, but aching for the companionship we had shared every day, two and three times in a day -- visiting on the telephone each morning, tea mug in hand, boiling water simmering on the stove, ready for the refills. Hour after hour our words flowed easily, the web of abiding friendship woven around cords of family, sharing appreciation of art, poetry, and nature, deeply caring about loving human kind, so keenly aware of the social inequities, encouraging one another, determining to reach beyond the barriers of prejudice and ignorance within our own families, workplaces, schools, churches -- such a tapestry that only Our Lord could weave -- the hues contrasting sharply when we dared to define LORD, his essence and his church.

We understood the "Call"; we were bound tightly with Forgiveness and Mercy, but torn to shreds on the "Rock". We kept "Heaven" and "Hell" on the fringes, allowing the Virgin Mary to keep us together as sisters -- an incredible friendship between Catholic and Protestant; yes, the Jonathan and David which we read about in different Bibles -- oh, the power of God's love.

"Mary, perhaps another time, another day," I faltered.

"Another day, another week, another lifetime. Dear Heart, what *more* have you got to lose?"

Only a sister could utter that question, and then tenderly offer the truthful answer.

"Your nineteen year marriage is finished, *finally*. You have lost your house, your *home*, Sue! And God only knows about your children *('Please, Blessed Mother, guide and protect them and bring them back to their mother who loves and needs them so much')*, your credit, your car, your cat, your dog ... and now your Health *('Please, God, that you keep her close to your Sacred Heart')*. She paused.

I was stunned. The truth of my entire adult life stated in a solitary sentence, uttered word for word by the friend who had seen me through each chapter of the journey. How many nights had I cried, "Why God? Where is the fairness in this union? Where is your mercy?" Now the doubts had crystallized into my choked words: "Abandoned " hanging astride the doctor's diagnosis of "Hypertension and a Potential Stroke." How many times had I prayed the Psalms, 'Hear me, Lord, answer me'? My mother's mother had died at age forty-six of a fatal stroke; my mother had recently sustained a stroke at fifty-two; my father was buried at the tender age of forty-two. Here I was, *forty-two*, completely alone and trying to absorb the inevitable -- my pending death with little hope of an afterlife, just an eternal sleep and the resurrection on Judgement Day.

Mary persisted, "They are nice people. The house is lovely, you'll appreciate it; and Sue, these are the people who have been praying for you for weeks. Remember I told you that I sat proxy for you."

"Thank you, Mary." I wondered if this really obligated me to something bigger. I could not finish my litany of reasons why I should say no to Mary, but with one final attempt I whispered:

"Mary, is this group, well, are they ... Catholic?" I hated Catholics, but Mary had been the exception. We had crossed over certain lines, fighting to maintain our "specialness" -- the term we understood to mean that God had blessed us.

"Well, of course."

I dared not ask, but formed the word, which I had never spoken, certain that the images would become a hideous reality.

"Mary, are they ... *Charismatic?*"

"Yes."

"Oh, GOD!!!"

"That's a good place to start."

How dare she? I knew my Bible so well. She knew my prejudice equally well. Catholic and Charismatic side-by-side the studious Protestant, the Christadelphian.

"What more do you have to lose?" Did she have to say the worst, the very thing we never agreed upon, ever.

"... your soul?"

There it was, spoken, out loud, up-front, between us. *"Dear God, Sweet Jesus! Oh, Mary ... my soul?"* Maybe this would be the shredding of our tapestry; but, what if, what if, just maybe, there was some truth that I did not know; a truth that she believed in so firmly that she was willing to strike cleanly, fully cognizant of my state of mind, my fragile health. Cheek to cheek with tears mingling, we wept; again and again, I whispered, "my *soul?* Oh, dear Mary, my *soul?*"

The night air was cool, hinting that spring was finally here. The drive through the fashionable neighborhood was quiet. Mary had been trying to remember the shortcut and I was trying not to remember her penetrating words, still stinging.

"Do you have your rosary beads?" She glanced over. "I remember when my other friend Susie had returned from Fatima, Portugal. She had just given me those beautiful beads. I had worked so late, had a patient in desperate trouble, so I went from

the hospital straight to church. I prayed knowing that you would
be moving, you know, into state housing, I mean your new house.
It was Mother's Day and you were walking before going to the
train. You were waiting for your son to come to pick you up and I
met you on the road. Remember?"

"Yes, I do remember." (How could he have left me and
without a car?)

"I reached into my pocket, prayed and kissed you, 'God be
with you. It's just for a short time'. I knew we would meet again,"
she continued, "but I knew that the Blessed Mother was telling me
to give you the rosary beads, that Susie and I were messengers, and
so the beads went from Fatima, to Susie, to me, and to you, Sue.
That's divine, I think. Providence. God's work, don't you think?"

I nodded, showing her the beautiful blue beads, which I had
placed under my pillow the first night and then stored them in a
bureau drawer for quite some time, maybe a year. I fingered them,
wondering if my Catholic grandmother had used beads like these.
"Fatima," Mary had said, "a place of miracles". I deliberately
placed them on my King James Bible, hoping that this evening
would end quickly and sensibly.

Assuring me again, Mary said, "They are nice people, you
will like them, except maybe one (he can be a bit much), but I just
know that this is going to be a *precious moment.*' " She smiled.

I nodded. I was bracing for the worst. Mary's promise of a
"special time in the Church," and now a "precious moment" --
these words forced a torrent of silent prayers. I begged God for
protection, for deliverance, for mercy, and all that it covered -- my
sins, my shame, my pain.

"Yes, Mary; the house is beautiful. (Had we finished our
house additions, had I had the opportunity to furnish the new
rooms: yes, Mary, the little dog, it is so much like mine; yes, the
children, very handsome; the hostess, so lovely and understated).
Amid the introductions and food, there was an air of expectancy.

Dishes were cleared away quickly, people moved into the family room, sitting on chairs and the floor; hymnbooks circulated and the guitar player strummed. I took a seat nearest the foyer just in case I might need to step out for air. Although the singing was enchanting, I tried to relax, but my body was shaking and the medicine was wearing off.

They begin praying the beads; I had opened my Bible, found the pages in the Psalms -- those faithful friends who had comforted me daily on the Boston train rides to the chic retail job in Copley Place. 'How odd,' I noted; 'how simply furnished this house was. Any of the homeowners in this neighborhood could easily have been my customer, shopping for expensive crystal and china, jewelry and art glass.' I lingered, dreaming of my lost home, my identity -- incredible that the Orrefors crystal bowl that I had won in a sales contest was now packed away in the damp house basement in a state project. I shuddered thinking that I would be forced to return to the little house. Fear was my constant companion; fear and the determination to move on and out -- yes, to another home, to a new life. Tonight could be a mere distraction, nothing more.

I shuddered again, unable to fathom my surroundings. Why was I crying and asking these people to "forgive me for hating them"; not really hating them, but hating everything that was Catholic, everything, that is, that *I thought* to be Catholic.

"Praise God." I recognized Rosaleen's voice, her eyes closed, hands outstretched. "Praise God, the scales of prejudice have been lifted." I scanned the room. Mary held me as my racked body heaved, whispering to me -- Pentecost.

I was too weak to move when they anointed my hands and head with oil, but I insisted on the Star of David, not the cross. Pentecost or not, some traditions should remain, I thought, and my upbringing was rooted in the Jewish promises, anchored on God's covenanted people. What was this language they were singing, praying? How presumptuous. How could they presume that the Lord would speak directly to certain individuals tonight, here in modern times? Yes, I believed that the Holy Spirit was the instrument of God, Jehovah, and I believed that the Holy Spirit had descended upon the Apostles, ushering in power to form the Lord's church, our Jewish brethren gratefully sharing the Promises, their Messiah, and the Good News with the Gentiles.

My God, these folks here were taking things into their own hands and I didn't intend to stay. If the Lord was going to speak to me, ever, it would definitely be through the Scriptures, not people. Immediately, in the depths of my heart I recalled Mary's invitation, "Come and See" -- so similar to Andrew's call to his brother, Peter: "Come and See." I shuddered again.

The following week Mary brought me again. I was not certain why I was willing to attend, perhaps other than to set a few things right within the Bible reading session. After the singing everyone had closed their eyes and chanted. Someone indicated that he or she was being led by the Holy Spirit to read a certain chapter of the Bible. (Incredible that the person needed assistance to locate the chapter.) Someone else attempted to explain the reading, to give an interpretation. It was more than I could bear. I sat watching, dismayed that, as a whole, this prayer group was not familiar with the Bible. I fought back my old prejudice, the one that smugly declared that they (Catholics) relied on priests to explain the "mysteries". The kindest thing I could do, and would do, was to gently correct any notions that didn't square with my understanding of truth. At least I could clarify any misunderstandings before leaving this group, and leave I would after the "being prayed over" business was done.

I caught a glimpse of the man as he came in the front door. Apparently, one or two others were pleased, seeing him quietly entering the foyer, heading to the kitchen. The hostess had been standing, waiting. Although the group had been attentive to me, they were now clearly excited, like children, anticipating a dessert after the meal. Immediately, they began anointing hands and head, and when I insisted on the Star of David, they looked at him; he nodded; they complied. I watched. So this was "the one who's a bit much at times" -- this was the Prophet.

I scanned him, head to toe; he certainly didn't look like a modern day evangelist to me. No suit, no clergy collar, just a smiling Irishman standing tall, in khakis and a wrinkled shirt, complete with sandals, needing a hair-cut, and definitely a manicure. Poor thing, look at his gnarled hands, oh the pain he must suffer. One by one they came to him, eager for his prayer; first the chanting, eyes closed; then, the silence, and finally, leaning over to speak privately to the eager recipient -- the word and the predictable nod of appreciation. I figured I could pass on this and remained in my seat, reading the Psalms and hoping Mary would not be long. Instead of our coats, Mary brought the man to me. "Don't be afraid," he said. "Just ask Jesus to come into your heart, silently."

Afraid? Suspicious was more like it. I started to get up but he was anointing me with his oil. Placing his hand on my head, he began chanting, praying and praying. Suddenly there was a circle of bodies. We were not alone and all these people had placed their hands on me, praying intently over *me*. He stopped; they stopped.

"The woman is looking for Truth." He leaned toward me, speaking quietly, "You have asked the Father to show you Truth, Pure Truth, to show you Himself."

Those were the words of my prayer, first thing every morning, riding into Boston; last thing every night. Word for word. "Lucky shot, Prophet," I thought, getting ready to rise.

He placed his hand on my head again. Prayed his funny chant and began. Speaking softly, "You have asked the LORD to give you a clean heart and a pure spirit." I reflected on this. I had not told Mary about these prayers and certainly not this one, because she was a nurse and I valued that knowledge as much as I craved a new spirituality. How did this stranger know the very words? Not merely content, but the actual words.

A third time, his hand on my head, he prayed a little longer than previously. I was about to bolt. There was a third prayer. "Please Lord, don't let him say it out loud, not publicly, *please* Lord." The second he stopped, I opened my eyes. He looked straight into mine, touched my shoulder and said nothing. He knew. We both knew the prayer, word for word. He turned to pray over Mary. Someone asked about the last prayer.

I wept. Surely God would never embarrass me. "Be ye perfect even as my Father is perfect." The Prophet had obeyed.

Mary was pleased that I agreed to come yet a third time. She met me there, as she intended to collect her daughter from an extracurricular activity. Everyone was chatting and visiting. I heard him before I saw him. Mary was telling him, "Frank, she knows her Bible." Mary Kate chimed in, "Yes, she does. Mrs. Tuzzo really knows her Bible."

Calmly he stated, "The woman is looking for Truth, Mary, Pure Truth."

"But she's not Catholic."

"She's in the right place, Mary; let God be God."

The Bible reading was about Moses and the burning bush. Easy enough, I thought. The group looked at me, waiting. They looked across the room at him, waiting. I said nothing, fingering the rosary beads, counting them to see if there really were fifty-three beads. My Psalm was 51; the beads, 53; the parable, 153 fish. Wouldn't it have been so neat to see how things sort of sit on top of each other like layers of color in the tapestry. But what was he asking? "Did we think that Moses really saw a burning bush? No? What burns and is never consumed?" I looked up from my reading, took a deep breath and waited for someone to take the bait. Suddenly, I could stand it no longer; he was impossible,

Moses and hot fudge sundaes.

"Did Moses actually see a burning bush? One would like to think so, wouldn't you?" If he was going to play spiritual ping-pong, we were off to a grand start. "Yes. One would like to think so. These are the words of God. That is what is written."

"The bush, the heart. Moses' heart, your heart …what burns with love and it is never consumed?"

The night was long and I had no interest in staying until the end. Here was the opportunity to make headway with the Bible teaching mission that I thought the Lord had given me and we were playing semantics with a foolish answer. I was glad that I had driven my own old car. I would head out as soon as possible. I whispered to Mary, explained that she was right: there was 'one that I might not like, a bit much,' to say the least. Please understand. Besides, my head ached -- dangerously so. I could feel every pulse and I was shaking so badly. Gathering my Bible, I leaned forward. Those sandals, the hands, the oil -- I didn't even ask for anything other than the cross on my hands and head. I was faint and needed air; but, politely, I waited while he prayed.

"Close the Book...."

I could barely believe what I was hearing. My God would never tell me to close the Bible. I had been weaned on Scriptures since I was a toddler. Years of Bible study, all the years of Sunday School, Bible vacation schools, Friday night classes, Sunday evening lectures -- a total focus on knowledge in order to worship. This was heresy.

"…and LIVE it." He moved on to the others in the next room. Everyone followed, but one.

"Forget it, Prophet. No, this is NOT from God; this is from the evil one!" I cried. Grabbing my jacket from the back of the chair, I bolted. Clearly, this was Heresy. I opened the door, running down the walkway, wondering where my car was parked. I slipped, exhausted, into the seat, turned on the ignition and eased out of the driveway, eager to be out of here forever. I slammed on my brakes, in total disbelief. The fog was so thick, I could not find the street. I could not see the end of my car. I left the engine running, walked back to the driveway, guiding my hands along the other cars. The lights were burning inside; I located the front door and banged on it with a closed fist.

"Open this door. Rosaleen, open this door," I shouted. Breathlessly facing my hostess, I sobbed, "I am LOST. I don't know the way." Everyone stared at him, amazed that he had just finished saying, "Don't worry. She'll be back. She is lost and doesn't know the way."

Kim stepped out of the house, stood beside me and said, "Come, follow me. I know the way. " We drove slowly, the fog, the rain, my tears all mingled into one blur, "Close the book and LIVE.... Come and See.... Come, Follow Me." Where had I heard these words?

Heavenly Father, Open My Heart
During the summer, I was getting sicker every day. My blood pressure was sky-rocketing; four medicines had failed to keep it "manageable". Ultrasounds, kidney scans, blood-flow test. The doctors were concerned, very concerned. There was the constant undercurrent of the dreaded Stroke, taking on a personality of its own. I didn't know if I cared any more about anything, not even my *soul*. Day after day passed, my working in Boston, then, walking all evening on the grounds of LaSalette with this John the Baptist. Maybe he wasn't a Prophet after all. Perhaps I would call him by his Christian name, but he walked so fast that I could barely keep up.

"What are you doing?"
"Praying...."
"Again?
"Hmm...."

"I mean, didn't you already do that? All day? Don't you ever grow weary of all this praying?

"... Listening to God."

"Francis! What is the point? The Beads, the Creed, the Stations, the Cross -- it's a constant flow. Every day is the same, more prayers and more meditation, daily Mass, sometimes twice; throw in a feast day or a saint's celebration, finish it up with an Hour or two; and of course, the torrent of telephone calls with the requests for -- you got it, another prayer! Walking Rosaries, Sitting Rosaries, Intercessory Rosaries, does it matter? Isn't it always the same? Don't you ever tire of it? The monotony? Don't you ever think about the things of this world?"

"I would love to check out. I can't wait. This life is so temporary. Heaven, that's the goal."

"Francis, how can you ever think like that? Did you forget that I'm the one dying?"

I didn't know which was faster, his walking gait or his prayers, but this routine was killing me. Trying to argue against every word of his precious "Hail, Mary" and walking so quickly, this would be the death of me. He thought we should try the Holy Stairs; not walking several flights of stairs, but slowly, one step at a time, kneeling and praying on each of the 'Twenty-Eight Holy Stairs.' Following behind, I noticed how difficult it was for this crippled man, so I started, slowly, word for word, "Our Father." Ten steps, I was finished. My body ached, but where was that man? I looked up and saw him kneeling under the crucifix, waiting patiently. Not once had I ever heard him complain; gently, he offered his handkerchief to my bloodied knees.

As the weeks passed, I was listening more, fathoming deeply the praise and hope in the "Hail Mary". Originally, this prayer had been open game, prey to my taunts of disbelief. Trusting every moment to the Lord, he listened and taught, corrected and reprimanded. It was agonizing for both of us, for he realized that I was a wounded child, and mother's milk was the only sustenance that I could tolerate. "Full of grace...." He dared to tread on sacred grounds, "You are more Catholic than you know."

"Having an Irish Catholic grandmother whose daughter was raised in the Church before her mother's death and subsequently marrying into and embracing a Protestant faith doesn't exactly qualify her as a full-fledged Catholic. In fact, I would not go so far as to say that I am a 'wanna be' just because I can recite the Rosary. So let's not go there."

Francis drove me to Boston College to visit with his Spiritual Director, Father Ronald Tacelli, who looked steadily at me. "Frank tells me that you want to be Catholic."

"Actually, sir, I want to study the Catholic faith and maybe someday, we can take it from there." He handed me a book by Frank Sheed and said he would call a priest friend to let him know that I was coming for Study.

The summer was ending and the operation, rapidly approaching. Francis drove me to the hospital again for the final test, the MRI, which would determine the details of the procedure. There had been several sophisticated tests and medicines, but my blood-pressure was dangerously elevated and still climbing. The fear of Stroke was indelibly etched in my being. Francis worked the beads as quickly as my heartbeat.

"Let's pray," he said as he eased into the handicap parking space by the lobby door.

I lost it -- every shred of decency and every ounce of gratitude, the haunting memories, the agony of no longer knowing, of questioning the beliefs rooted in a lifetime of study -- I lost it, hysterical.

"What?!! Another Hail Mary, another Glory Be!"

"Susan, I have prayed. Everything will be all right. It's okay. Let's pray for the graces and give thanks."

"Graces!" I screamed. *"I am facing my death ... my family history. I never knew my grandmother (and don't tell me that she is praying for me)! Forty-two, I am forty-two and dying ... and I don't KNOW anything anymore, nothing! You talk about graces, GRACES! I don't want Graces, I want OUT!"* I slammed the car door so hard, but I didn't care if the door was damaged. I was broken. Completely, unequivocally broken.

The young man met me in the lobby. I was breathless and could barely speak. He took a moment, letting me collect myself. "Susan, do you know why you are here today?"

"I am having an operation. The doctors need another test."

"I see. Do you know why?"

"I'm here on faith."

"A Christian?"

"Trying to be ... but...."

We exited the hospital corridors, crossed the lot and entered into a little mobile unit. He explained the procedure, instructing me to remove all jewelry, no metal allowed once inside the tube. I stood in front of the table, taking in its dimensions and that of the tube. A casket, I thought, a casket being carried a cave. Death, finally. I thought about my children, "Where did I fail?" I remembered the whole crazy summer and lay down on the table. Music? Something soft, please, exiting music. I thought about Francis, knowing he would be praying, walking the parking lot and working those beads. I cringed at my outburst, "graces". Whatever. It didn't matter. I didn't think I cared and then the pounding started. Picture after picture; a minute to rest while the technician changed the film. The darkness -- I wondered if I could reach my tongue to the inside of the tube casing. "Don't breathe; hold still, focus on something pleasant."

Two-and-one-half hours later, the technician offered to walk me back to the lobby.

"Susan, do you know why you are here?"

"What? Again, please?"

"Do you know why you are here?"

I was astounded. Hadn't we had this questioning earlier?

"You have two doctors," he continued. Neither one of them has told you that they are looking for a tumor on your kidney and adrenal gland. It is shutting off the circulation to your heart."

"No."

"Do you want to tell me what you have done? I have seen your chart. I just viewed your pictures. They are absolutely perfect." He waited.

I breathed as deeply as I could.

"It's important to give praise to God."

"I claimed ... I asked the Blessed Mother ... to heal me and that if she did, I would believe and I would tell others, always about the mercy of God." I opened my hand. The beautiful blue beads, metal chain and cross, tiny beads for a small child -- held in my hand the entire time that I was in the Casket.

"Your doctors will not call you again. You must believe. Go in faith and know that you have been healed."

We entered the lobby and desperately I tried to fathom what had happened. I stammered, "What is your name? Tell me." (Imagine needing credibility in the midst of a miracle). I was so afraid to imagine such a blessing after such sinfulness.

"My name is Stephen. Go in peace, and learn about the Holy Spirit."

As I brushed away the tears from my chin, I turned. He was gone.

"Thomas, thrust your hand into mine, your hand into my side. Doubt no more. Blessed are those who have not seen and believe."

"Francis. I must find him, to tell him. Francis, please accept my apologies, I am so sorry." I rushed to the car and it was empty. I ran around the parking lots, front and back, but he was nowhere to be found. I closed my eyes and prayed, looked up. There, the hill in the distance. Stumbling on the rough terrain, I wondered how a man crippled with arthritis and wearing sandals could manage such a steep climb. "Where, God? Where could he be?"

Kneeling under the tree, rosary in hand -- the Prophet. I knelt beside him.

"God heard your prayer."

"And yours."

"Hail Mary, full of grace...."

"Blessed are you among women...."

" ... and blessed is the fruit of thy womb, Jesus. Father Casey. Will you take me?"

Saturday after Saturday, we drove to Campion Center in Weston, Massachusetts, home to the Jesuits. Father Joseph Casey had never received the call from Father Tacelli, but he considered it "an honor to be a priest and to share the Faith". Appreciative of the details of my recent journey, he was more curious about my background (Protestant and well-versed in the Bible), but how did I come so well-prepared in the Catholic basics? Had I been through a formal program?

"No, Father. I have spent several grueling months with a Prophet."

"A prophet? You mean a priest?"

"No, Father. I mean a fierce Irish man who takes his Roman Catholic faith to life, to each and every moment of his life. A man who loves his God more than life itself, a man who trusts so completely in God that he never worries about details. Absolutely Nothing. *Father, He not only takes every concern to prayer, but then he leaves it in the hands of God.* No fears, no complaints, just humility and obedience. Francis is a Prayer Warrior who wants nothing more than for every man to Love God with all his heart and mind. He lives what he prays and the Lord God answers him."

"A lay man? A layman with such a devout prayer life and trust... But Susan, you do not know God. You know your scriptures, but you cannot me tell who was Jesus?"

This sounded vaguely familiar. First assignment: "Choose a gospel, any one, except John."

"John is my favorite."

"Really? John knew. You don't. Prove the identity of God. Who did Jesus say that He was?"

"Prove the identity of God." Amazing how the Holy Spirit worked. The very verses that I might have drawn upon to disprove the Trinity were the very ones that converted me.

"Holy Spirit, Soul of my Soul, I Adore Thee.
Guide Me, Encourage Me, Comfort Me, Console Me.
Command me to do Thy Will,
That I may submit to all that Thou permit to happen to me,
Only that I may Know Thy Will."

Nine months and two weeks from my first Catholic thing, Pentecost, Father Casey baptized me, confirmed me, and celebrated my first Holy Communion -- Truth-filled sacraments in one precious moment. Easter New Life.

"What name will you take?"

"Mary Frances."

"Susan Grace Mary Frances Tuzzo. That's a lot of names. Shall we drop the Grace?"

I laughed. "Drop the Grace? Father, it has taken me forty-two years to grow in Grace. No, Father, Grace remains. We could drop the surname for a sacramental marriage, but for the moment, it's Susan Grace Mary Frances Tuzzo."

"Yes. In the name of the Father, the Son, and the Holy Spirit. Amen."

" ... Only say but the word and my *soul* shall be healed."

(Susan Grace Mary Frances Tuzzo)

A Gentle Servant of God

I first met Frank Kelly when I was invited by a common friend, Rosaleen, to come to her house and attend a prayer group that she and her husband, Jim, used to have at their house in Norfolk, Massachusetts. Jim, Rosaleen, and I were friends, and they invited me to give the teaching that night at their prayer group and to pray over people for healing at the end. That was something that I used to do and I continue to do to the present day.

As I was praying over Frank, the Holy Spirit gave me knowledge of the gentleness and sincerity of this man. I didn't know his story, but the Spirit was certainly anointing him.

Frank has always been a gentle servant of God, humble and sincere. On one occasion I asked him to pray over me, and I felt how the Lord was pleased to use him as a vessel to minister to other people. His words and his prayerfulness were both inspiring. That is how I always think of him when I pray for him, as a gentle servant of God.

(Fr. Francisco "Paco" Anzoategui)

Endorsement from Eluru about Word of Knowledge of Healing

I am a Catholic priest from the diocese of Eluru in southern India. I have been associated with Mr. Francis B. Kelly, whom we call "Frank" affectionately, for the last fifteen years. He is a great friend of our diocese. Year after year, he has made his house a home for the missionary priests from our diocese who go to the archdiocese of Boston to preach mission appeals. I have had the opportunity of being in his house several times over the years. At first, my relationship with him was one of friendship. He allowed me to make fun with him. He was like a little child. He used to take us along with him for some prayer meetings and pray over the people. He also used to pray over the telephone quoting biblical references. I was among those who used to [try to] fool him.

When I was in his house in the summer of 1999, my Bishop telephoned me and informed me that my youngest sister was sick and her condition was not good. I was sad. I went into the upper room (a make-shift chapel in Frank's house) and started praying. Frank returned home from the city and was surprised to see me sad in the chapel. He put his hand over my head and asked me if there was something wrong. I said there wasn't anything. He then prayed over me for a while and told me that I was sad because my sister was admitted to the hospital and she was not well. What he said was a shock to me. I wondered how he could know this. He told me not to worry and prayed over me again and told me that my sister was alright. A few minutes later, my brother called me and told me that she was getting better. Since then, my entire perspective about Frank has changed. I could no longer [try to] fool him. I began to discover a holy man in Frank. I began to experience a special power in the form of heat (electricity) in his hands when he prayed over me. I began to appreciate the special gift God gave him in bringing His comforting presence to the people.

(Fr. P. Bala, Procurator, Diocese of Eluru)

130

Blessings from Bishop (Excerpt from Letter)

Dear Frank,

.... God bless you and your apostolate.

I had the opportunity to see the video tape and come to know how God is using you for the renewal of His people. I wish you fruitful ministry and my prayers are with you! I am sure that I will have the chance of meeting you again. Your life of faith and prayer, love and service, impressed me and inspired me!

I request you to pray for me and for my diocese. I need God's grace and His Wisdom to carry on with my ministry.

Wishing you well and invoking God's blessings. Yours affectionately in the Lord.

(Most Rev. Mallabarapu Prakash, D.D.
Bishop, Diocese of Vijayawada, India)

✝

Frank Kelly's Teaching on the Gifts of the Holy Spirit and the Charisms

St. Paul told the Corinthians that there are indeed "higher gifts" (1 Corinthians 12:31). Now the Church has recognized many gifts to build up the Body of Christ. On the one hand, there are the foundational gifts designed for each of the faithful and received at Baptism (and then Confirmation): Wisdom, Understanding, Counsel, Fortitude, Knowledge, Piety, and Fear of the Lord (see Isaiah 11:2-3).

But these differ from those we call "charismatic gifts" or "charisms", some of which include the following: prophecy, discernment of spirits, angelical prayer (tongues), interpretation of tongues, teaching with faith, wisdom in discourse, utterance of knowledge, miracles, and healing (see 1 Corinthians 12:1-11). By contrast with the seven universal gifts of the Holy Spirit enumerated above, the Holy Spirit gives these particular charisms as He wills (see 1 Corinthians 12:11). This is why we call the Holy Spirit "the Lord and Giver of Life" in the Nicene Creed at Mass on Sunday. This is also why we pray with the psalmist in Psalm 51:10, *RSV*: "Create in me a clean heart, O God, and put a new and right spirit within me."

Let us briefly examine the gifts that God has given to complete the action of the virtues and that Providence has disposed for both the individual and the common good.

Wisdom

Wisdom is perhaps the most noble of gifts simply because

it is through Wisdom that one understands more deeply the truths of the Faith. With the gift of Wisdom, one is more fully able to respond to God's love and the working of His grace. Wisdom keeps the pious soul humble, causing one to wonder at the marvels of the Creator. Wisdom is responsible mainly for the unusual awareness of one's own sins or the sins of the world. On account of Wisdom the saints offered themselves up to God in reparation for sin, becoming victim souls of God's enduring love. All we have to offer are our own pain and sinfulness -- but God can accomplish much with that. Some saints with a notable possession of Wisdom include St. Francis Xavier, St. Anthony Mary Claret, and the Doctors of the Church.

The charisms associated with Wisdom are the interpretation of tongues and teaching with faith in the Holy Spirit (rather than through academic learning).

Understanding

The gift of Understanding is closely related to Wisdom. This gift helps us to penetrate profound divine truths more easily and quickly. This condition normally occurs in the state of illumination, whereby God imparts Understanding to the intellect without any effort on the part of the recipient person. In fact, what is learned about the divine mysteries in this state of illumination often occurs in a brief moment of time, resulting in an understanding that exceeds what one can do through a lifetime of study and meditation. This gift is promised by Christ also in Matthew 5:8: "Blessed are the pure in heart, for they shall see God."

Saints noted for the gift of Understanding were the four Evangelists (Sts. Matthew, Mark, Luke, and John) and St. Anselm of Canterbury.

The charism associated with Understanding is the

discernment of spirits.

Knowledge

The gift of Knowledge gives us the ability to see everything from a supernatural or divine perspective. Thus, it is helpful toward recognizing the follies of the world, while eagerly awaiting the glory of Heaven. Knowledge makes us aware of and sorry for past sins. It helps us get rid of the things preventing our spiritual growth. One fruit of this gift is consolation during times of doubt. As it is written in Matthew 5:4, "Blessed are those who mourn, for they shall be comforted."

Some saints remarkable for the gift of Knowledge were St. Catherine of Sienna, St. Dominic, and St. Alphonsus Liguori.

The charism associated with Knowledge is prophecy (which, by the way, should be short and scriptural).

Counsel

The gift of Counsel prepares those who are called to give advice or spiritual direction to a needy soul. It also helps us to know what actions are right to take in a given situation, especially those actions which reflect justice, mercy, and love. It is closely related to the virtue of prudence, which directs us in making responsible and orderly judgments about our thoughts or deeds. If someone is not suffering and praying, that person should be avoided as a counselor.

Some saints with a special gift of Counsel were St. Francis de Sales, St. Teresa of Avila, and St. Thérèse of Lisieux.

The charisms associated with Counsel are wisdom in discourse and healing.

Piety

Piety is a gift that gives one reverence for the Father as our God and Creator. Piety intensifies our adoration of God and our veneration of all that is holy (particularly the angels and saints). Because Piety increases our love for God, it in turn increases our love for neighbor in imitation of Jesus. Since He died for us, we must die for Him and our neighbor. Piety shows us how to depend on God in order to work through word and deed. Thus, Piety and charity are interrelated, whereby one influences the other.

Some saints exemplary for Piety were St. Monica, St. Rita, and St. Francis of Assisi.

The charisms associated with Piety are praying in tongues and utterance of knowledge for instruction.

Fortitude

Fortitude, as a gift of the Holy Spirit, gives us supernatural strength to accomplish things that we could normally not do through our own human efforts (for example, fight off the devil and temptation). Fortitude helps us to overcome difficult obstacles and to endure throughout our hardships. Many of the saints had difficult encounters with the evil one; they had to rely upon their faith with proper discernment in order to win these spiritual battles.

Some outstanding models of Fortitude are St. Benedict and St. Padre Pio.

The charism associated with Fortitude is the working of miracles to promote the fruit of perseverance.

Fear of the Lord

Fear of the Lord is the first step to Wisdom (see Job 28:28;

Psalm 111:10; Proverbs 15:33; Sirach 1:14, 20, 27). This is a gift to show us that God created everything and to help us to live everything for the Will of God. Whatever we do, we do it in unity with God and to give glory to Him.

Some saints to contemplate regarding Fear of the Lord are St. Joseph, St. Peter, St. Paul, all the Apostles, and St. Bernard.

The charism associated with Fear of the Lord is wisdom in discourse.

✝

Appendix I
Pope John Paul II on the Charismatic Gifts

(Reprinted by *The Wanderer*, July 23, 1992, from *L'Osservatore Romano*, English language edition, July 1, 1992.)

Charisms Have Role In Church's Life

(In his general audience of June 24, 1992, Pope John Paul II explained to his listeners that God gives each of us gifts appropriate to our particular mission. These gifts are meant to be used for the good of the Church and for the good of each other.)

"It is not only through the sacraments and the ministrations of the Church that the Holy Spirit makes holy the People of God, leads them, and enriches them with His virtues. Allotting His gifts as He wills (cf. I *Cor.* 12:11), He also distributes special graces among the faithful of every rank. By these gifts He makes them fit and ready to undertake various tasks and offices for the renewal and building up of the Church" (*Lumen Gentium*, n. 12). This is the teaching of the Second Vatican Council.

Therefore, the People of God's sharing in the messianic mission is not obtained only through the Church's ministerial structure and sacramental life. It also occurs in another way, that of the spiritual gifts or charisms.

This doctrine, recalled by the Council, is based on the New Testament and helps to show that the development of the ecclesial community does not depend only on the institution of ministries and sacraments, but is also furthered by the free and unforeseeable gifts of the Spirit, who works outside established channels, too.

Because of this bestowal of special graces it is apparent that the universal priesthood of the ecclesial community is led by the Spirit with a sovereign freedom ("as He wishes," St. Paul says [I *Cor.* 12:11]) that is often amazing.

St. Paul describes the variety and diversity of the charisms, which must be attributed to the work of the one Spirit (I *Cor.* 12:4).

Each of us receives from God many gifts which are appropriate for us personally and for our mission. Because of this diversity, no individual way of holiness or mission is ever identical to another. The Holy Spirit shows respect for each person and wants to foster in each one an original development of the spiritual life and the giving of witness.

Gifts are Bestowed for the Church's Benefit

But we must keep in mind that spiritual gifts are to be accepted not only for one's personal benefit, but above all for the good of the Church: "As each one," St. Peter writes, "has received a gift, use it to serve one another as good stewards of God's varied grace" (I *Pt.* 4:10).

Because of these charisms, the community's life is full of spiritual wealth and every kind of service. And diversity is necessary for a greater spiritual wealth: everyone makes a personal contribution which the others do not. The spiritual community lives on the contribution of all.

The diversity of charisms is also necessary for a better ordering of the entire life of the Body of Christ. St. Paul emphasizes this when he explains the purpose and usefulness of the spiritual gifts: "You are Christ's Body, and individually parts of it" (I *Cor.* 12:27).

In the one Body each person must fulfill his own role in accord with the charism he has received. No one can claim to have received all the charisms, nor can he allow himself to be jealous of the charisms of others. Each person's charism must be respected and appreciated for the good of the Body.

A Proper Discernment of Charisms is Essential

It should be noted that charisms require discernment, especially in the case of extraordinary charisms.

This discernment is given by the same Holy Spirit, who guides the intellect along the way of truth and wisdom. But since the whole ecclesial community has been placed by Christ under the leadership of the ecclesiastical authority, this latter is responsible for judging the value and authenticity of the charisms.

The Council says: "Extraordinary gifts are not to be rashly desired, nor is it from them that the fruits of apostolic labors are to be presumptuously expected. Those who have charge over the Church should judge the genuineness and proper use of these gifts, through their office not indeed to extinguish the Spirit, but to test all things and hold fast to what is good (cf. I *Thes.* 5:12, 19-21)" (*Lumen Gentium*, n. 12).

Some generally followed criteria of discernment can be indicated both by the ecclesiastical authority or by spiritual masters and directors:

a) *Agreement with the Church's faith in Jesus Christ* (cf. I *Cor.* 12:3). A gift of the Holy Spirit cannot be contrary to the faith which the same Spirit inspires in the whole Church. "This is how," St. John writes, "you can know the Spirit of God: Every spirit that acknowledges Jesus Christ come in the flesh belongs to God, and every spirit that does not acknowledge Jesus does not belong to God" (I *John* 4:2).

b) *The presence of the "fruit of the Spirit: love, joy, peace"* (*Gal.* 5:22). Every gift of the Spirit fosters growth in love, both in the person himself and in the community, and thus it produces joy and peace.

If a charism causes trouble and confusion, this means either that it is not genuine or that it has not been used in the right way. As St. Paul says: "He is not the God of disorder but of peace" (I *Cor.* 14:33).

Without love, even the most extraordinary charisms are not at all useful (cf. I *Cor.* 13:1-3; see also *Mt.* 7:22-23).

c) *Conformity with the Church's authority* and acceptance of its directives. After laying down very strict rules for using charisms in the Church of Corinth, St. Paul says: "If anyone thinks that he is a prophet or a spiritual person, he should recognize that what I am writing to you is a commandment of the Lord" (I *Cor.* 14:37). The authentic charismatic is recognized by his sincere docility to the pastors of the Church. A charism cannot cause rebellion or a rupture of unity.

d) *The use of charisms* in the community is subject to a simple rule: "Everything should be done for building up" (I *Cor.* 14:26), i.e., charisms are accepted to the extent that they make a constructive contribution to the life of the community, a life of union with God and of fraternal communion. St. Paul insists firmly on this rule (I *Cor.* 14:4-5, 12, 18-19, 26-32).

Freedom of Speech in the Church Can Be Beneficial

Among the various gifts, St. Paul holds that of prophecy in such high esteem, as we noted, that he recommends: "Strive eagerly for the spiritual gifts, above all that you may prophesy" (I *Cor.* 14:1). It appears from the history of the Church and particularly from the lives of the saints that frequently the Holy Spirit inspires prophetic words meant to foster the development or the reform of the Christian community's life. Sometimes these words are addressed especially to those who wield authority, as in the case of St. Catherine of Siena, who intervened with the Pope to obtain his return from Avignon to Rome. There are many faithful and, above all, many saints who have given Popes and other pastors of the Church the light and strength necessary for fulfilling their mission, especially at difficult times for the Church.

This fact shows the possibility and usefulness of freedom of speech in the Church: a freedom which can also appear in the form of constructive criticism. The important thing is that what is said truly expresses a prophetic inspiration coming from the Spirit. As St. Paul says, "where the Spirit of the Lord is, there is freedom" (II *Cor.* 3:17). The Holy Spirit fosters in the faithful a manner of acting characterized by sincerity and mutual trust (cf. *Eph.* 4:25) and enables them "to admonish one another" (*Rom.* 15:14; cf. *Col.* 1:16).

Criticism is useful in the community, which must always be reformed and must try to correct its own imperfections. In many cases it helps the community to take a new step forward.

But if it comes from the Holy Spirit, criticism must be animated by the desire to advance in truth and love. It cannot be given with bitterness; it cannot be expressed in insults, in acts or judgments which offend the honor of individuals or groups.

It must be filled with respect and with fraternal and filial affection, and it should avoid recourse to inappropriate words or publicity by always adhering to the directions given by the Lord about fraternal correction (cf. *Mt.* 18:15-16).

If this is the profile of freedom of speech, we can say that there is no opposition between charism and institution, because it is the one Spirit who enlivens the Church with the various charisms. The spiritual gifts also help in exercising the ministries. They are bestowed by the Spirit to help advance the Kingdom of God. In this sense we can say that the Church is a community of charisms.

✝

Appendix 2
St. Thomas Aquinas on the Gratuitous Gifts
(by David P. Lang)

St. Thomas Aquinas is considered the "Common" (or "Universal") Doctor of the Catholic Church. In other words, the Church regards his teaching as safe to follow in nearly every aspect of dogmatic and moral theology that he discusses. He employs a logical method of argument (sound philosophical reasoning) to arrive at his conclusions, in order to help us understand the "why" of the answers he gives to important questions.

An ardent champion of Aquinas was Pope Leo XIII. Lauding St. Thomas with glowing terms in his encyclical *Aeterni Patris*, Pope Leo states that "he is rightly and deservedly esteemed the special bulwark and glory of the Catholic Faith" and that "reason, borne on the wings of Thomas to its human height, can scarcely rise higher, while faith could scarcely expect more or stronger aids from reason than those which she has already obtained through Thomas". Pope John Paul II ratifies the judgment of Pope Leo XIII in his own encyclical *Fides et Ratio*, declaring that in St. Thomas "the Church's Magisterium has seen and recognized the passion for truth". Pope John Paul calls Aquinas an "apostle of the truth", quoting Pope Paul VI's apostolic letter *Lumen Ecclesiae* ("Light of the Church", issued in 1974 during the seventh centenary year after the Universal Doctor's entrance into heavenly glory).

St. Thomas is also called the "Angelic Doctor", probably for several reasons: (1) the purity of his life that was so conducive to the acquisition of wisdom; (2) his soaring intellect that (like the angelic mind) seemed capable of penetrating the deepest mysteries about God and creation; (3) his peerless (in both quantity and quality) writings on the angels, providing us lesser mortals a glimpse into the nature and activities of these wondrous finite spiritual entities.

With such a towering genius as Aquinas at our disposal, it is not surprising that we should be curious about what he has to say regarding the charismatic gifts. He does indeed elaborate at some length (as usual) on what he calls these "gratuitous graces". We need only consult Part I-II, Question 111, and Part II-II, Questions 171-178, of his monumental *Summa Theologica* -- a revered treasure in the Church's heritage of sublime literature produced by the canonized saints.

The Meaning of Gratuitous Grace

St. Thomas stresses that sanctifying grace is nobler than any gratuitous grace, because sanctifying grace is more directly related to the goal of eternal salvation, whereas a charismatic gift is merely an instrumental aid to salvation and not necessarily a sign of holiness. He defines a "gratuitous grace" as a divine gift bestowed to help lead others to God. But no one except God can directly move another person's interior acts of intellect and will; at most, a human being can influence or persuade through outward teaching. The gratuitous gifts supply these various external means for the purpose of instruction in matters beyond natural human reasoning. Now in order to instruct another, someone must first have adequate knowledge. Second, in order to be even more effective, the teacher must be able to confirm what is taught. Third, the teacher must have the capacity to get across God's message in a suitable fashion.

With respect to the first requirement (namely, adequate knowledge), three qualities are needed: *faith* (zealous certitude about the principles of Catholic doctrine), *word of wisdom* (firm understanding of the chief conclusions that follow regarding divine matters), and *word of knowledge* (the overt ability to show concretely how these effects apply to human affairs).

With respect to the second requirement (namely, confirmation), it is fitting for the teacher to perform signs manifesting divine power. In one way, he might reveal what only God can know: either through *prophecy* (foretelling contingent future events) or through *discernment* (reading interior secrets of the soul). In another way, he might do what only God can accomplish: either through *working miracles* (in the outer physical world) or through *healing* (restoring inner bodily health).

With respect to the third requirement (namely, suitable speech), the teacher may display the gift of *tongues* or the gift of *interpretation of tongues*.

In another place, Aquinas lists the charismatic gifts under several headings: prophecy, word of wisdom and knowledge, tongues (which may require interpretation), and miracles (including healing). Although these differ in definition, they are interrelated. In itself prophecy primarily consists in knowledge granted by special divine illumination. Secondarily, though, the prophet uses the words of speech to communicate his divine enlightenment for the sake of instructing others. This speech may involve foreign languages, in which case interpretation is needed. Furthermore, prophecy may be accompanied by miracles to prove or confirm the divine origin of the prophet's utterances. We will treat each of the charisms in this list one-by-one.

Prophecy

Clarifying the meaning of prophecy, Aquinas makes some distinctions. Since the prophet is one who speaks what God wants revealed, St. Thomas asserts that prophecy may extend to any conceivable knowledge. But clearly the kind of knowledge most properly associated with prophecy concerns matters that are difficult for human beings (as such) to attain. After all (we might note), if someone announces new scientific facts achieved through observation and experimentation or new mathematical theorems arrived at by deduction from premises, we don't typically view him as a prophet, because these matters are discoverable through unaided human reasoning. Instead, genuine prophecy in the customary sense discloses more remote and lofty knowledge exceeding natural human capacities.

Prophecy varies in status according to its extent of elevation beyond the reach of human knowledge. There are three levels here, each one ranking above the preceding in excellence.

(1) Some prophetic knowledge surpasses what a particular individual naturally knows through sensory experience and intellectual processes, but does not exceed what others can naturally know. For instance, it would be prophetic for a cloistered nun confined to a convent without the resources of newspapers, telephone, radio, television, or computer network to know what is currently happening in another country, but it would *not* necessarily be prophetic for that country's inhabitants themselves to know about the same occurrences. (Aquinas gives as a Scriptural illustration 2 Kings 5:25-26.) Another example at this level is knowledge of hidden thoughts. If these are communicated to others verbally (orally or by writing), then obviously no prophecy is involved. But a prophet may "read" the "thoughts of the heart" without such media. (See 1 Corinthians 14:24-25.)

(2) A superior degree of prophecy encompasses truths that no human being is naturally capable of knowing, yet truths that are supremely intelligible in themselves. An example is the exalted mystery of the Blessed Trinity, which must be accepted on faith in order to deliver the inner conviction of certitude. (This dogma is foreshadowed in Isaiah 6:3, but more explicitly revealed in Matthew 28:19 and Galatians 4:6.)

(3) Finally, some matters are removed from the very possibility of natural knowledge on account of their intrinsic unknowability: namely, future contingencies. Of course, God knows such events infallibly, since He embraces (and controls) all time as simultaneously present in the permanently abiding or changeless gaze of His eternal Mind. Hence, if God chooses to reveal them, the prophetic light is at its peak of intensity in the recipient who foretells these future events with exactitude. (We think of the Old Testament prophets Moses, David, Isaiah, Jeremiah, Ezekiel, Daniel, Joel, Zechariah, *et cetera*. And then there is the famous prophet of conditional chastisement that does not materialize -- Jonah.)

But we should note that, due to the weakness of the prophet's mind, the divine certitude about such matters is not necessarily adequately reflected in the prophet, who may grasp them in an unsteady or hesitant manner. (This applies to private revelations, where God may permit the messages to be filtered to the point of distortion when the prophet attempts to express them in words.) Moreover, even if the prophet does apprehend them firmly, he need not comprehend them exhaustively with all their ramifications. An example of this might be Caiaphas' pronouncement before Christ's capture that it was better for one man to die for the people (see John 11:49-51).

Aquinas further subdivides prophecy into *denunciation, predestination,* and *foreknowledge.* The prophecy of denunciation foretells a conditional relation of cause to effect, and hence is not always fulfilled (for example, the destruction of Nineveh in the book of Jonah). The prophecy of predestination foretells what God will inevitably bring about by His own wisdom, goodness, and power (such as the resurrection of the dead at the end of the world). The prophecy of foreknowledge predicts what will happen as a result of the operation of human free-will (such as the denial of Jesus by St. Peter and His betrayal by Judas).

In all cases, says St. Thomas, prophetic knowledge is bestowed on man via a divine enlightenment. Nevertheless, the Angelic Doctor declares that this illumination is conveyed to men by the ministry of angels.

Throughout his treatise on prophecy (in Questions 171-175), Aquinas uses many illustrations drawn from Sacred Scripture. Yet he does not restrict the gift of prophecy to the Biblical era, after which public revelation ended. For he includes the reality of private revelation by stating that "at all times there have not been lacking persons having the spirit of prophecy, not indeed for the declaration of any new doctrine of faith, but for the direction of human acts." (In this regard we recall the Church-approved apparitions of the Queen of Prophets to seers at Guadalupe, LaSalette, Fatima, and Akita -- as well as prophesying saints and blesseds such as St. Vincent Ferrer, Bl. Anna Maria Taigi, and St. Padre Pio.)

Word of Wisdom and Knowledge

St. Thomas reminds us that God gives the charisms for the sake of helping others. But knowledge of divine things cannot be transmitted to this end without speech. In order for instruction to prove effective, the Holy Spirit furnishes the gifts of the *word*. As a result, hearers are taught intellectually, moved emotionally, and influenced in their wills to do what is right.

Aquinas closely links the gift of prophecy with the gifts of the word and with certain other gratuitous graces.

When prophetic knowledge pertains directly to mankind, it concerns future events -- at least in some way. It may be either actual foreknowledge or else knowledge of present hidden things having consequences for the future. Such knowledge is imparted in order to guide or direct our actions for our benefit. Hence, St. Thomas subsumes the gifts of the *word of wisdom* and *word of knowledge* under the generic heading of prophecy. They are differentiated as we have already seen. The *word of wisdom* ensures a firm understanding of the chief conclusions that follow from the central doctrines of the Catholic Church, so that the teacher can accurately and zealously share the Faith with others. On the other hand, the *word of knowledge* endows the prophet with the overt ability to show concretely how these consequences apply to particular practical human affairs. The word of knowledge evidently supplements the word of wisdom, so that wisdom does not remain on the plateau of mere theory.

Sometimes, however, the knowledge manifested through the prophet bears a connection with angels. Since these beings may influence mankind either for good or for evil, we need to know how to distinguish these two possibilities. Thus, the Angelic Doctor puts the gift of *discernment of spirits* under the overall heading of prophecy (see 1 Thessalonians 5:19-22).

Finally, prophetic knowledge may pertain essentially to God. On the one hand, such knowledge may comprise those truths inaccessible to human reasoning that must be accepted as part of the traditional deposit of the Faith. Once we hear these things proclaimed, while understanding that they are being proposed unconditionally as necessary facets of Catholic identity, we must believe them at peril of our salvation. But, on the other hand, some knowledge about God transcends these doctrines to open up vistas on more detailed truths that are not part of the Creed. Though not demanding the assent of faith, they enrich the recipient with a more perfect or complete wisdom. (The distinction between public and private revelation seems to be implied here. For example, First Friday devotions to the Sacred Heart of Jesus and First Saturday devotions to Our Lady of Mount Carmel of Fatima through the Rosary and Brown Scapular are not proposed by the Church for acceptance on Divine and Catholic faith as absolutely necessary for salvation -- unlike the obligation to attend Mass on Sundays. Yet it

150

would exhibit folly or a lack of wisdom to dismiss these practices as valuable ways to increase in grace and thereby aid one's salvation.) We should comment, though, that the gratuitous charisms of *faith* and *wisdom* exceed in intensity the ordinary supernatural virtue of faith and the Holy Spirit's infused gift of wisdom. The charisms consist in such a zealous and irrepressible certitude about the principles and conclusions of Catholic doctrine that the charismatic effects become outwardly visible in the prophet's deeds. One might deem the prophet to be on fire with divine truth -- a fire that cannot help but spread the word.

Tongues

By the gift of "tongues", St. Thomas means primarily (if not exclusively) what can be defined as *glossolalia* in the strict sense -- the ready ability to speak actual foreign languages fluently without any previous course of instruction. The two purposes of this gift are teaching the Faith to a diversity of peoples and praising God.

The classic example of this phenomenon is, of course, the Pentecost event recorded in Acts 2:4-12, where it is reported that the Apostles "began to speak in other tongues, as the Holy Spirit gave them utterance", so that a multitude of people from various nations all heard the Apostles in their own native languages. Perhaps these verses record, not merely a miracle of internal *hearing* performed within the gathered crowd, but the prodigy of actually *speaking* foreign languages externally on the part of the Apostles. We will speculate below about whether anything more than the strict meaning of glossolalia might be included in the charism of "tongues".

Aquinas explains that the gift of prophecy is more splendid than the gift of tongues, for several reasons. First, the gift of tongues concerns only the knowledge of words, which occupy a lower rung in the scale of reality than truths in the prophet's mind and the things to which the prophet's knowledge refers under divine illumination. Second, the gift of prophecy is more advantageous for the Church than the gift of tongues. For unless the strange speech is interpreted (which comes under the gift of prophecy), there is no edification for others (whether members of the Church or not) -- nor possibly even for the prophet himself. (See St. Paul's lengthy amplification in 1 Corinthians 14:3-33.) Third, the prophet is related to God mentally, which is nobler than a merely verbal relation to God through speaking in tongues. Fourth, by prophecy someone is connected with both God and man, whereas the gift of tongues establishes a link only with God to the exclusion of others (absent interpretation).

How about the seemingly unintelligible repetition of syllables that characterizes most contemporary manifestations of so-called "tongues"? Of course, some of this "speech" may contain genuine words or entire sentences from actual human languages that happen to be unknown to the speaker. Such cases would embody, at least partially, instances of glossolalia. Furthermore, even known languages sometimes contain meaningless concatenations of syllables expressing pure emotion (such as "zippety-doo-dah-zippety-ay"). Yet so much of this "speech" seems to consist in a gibberish chatter or a sing-song hum. Would the Angelic Doctor judge this apparent nonsense to be an authentic display of the gift of tongues? Unfortunately, he does not explicitly discuss this issue in his treatise on the charismatic gifts.

Nevertheless, invoking 1 Corinthians 14:2, Aquinas does say that one who speaks in tongues speaks directly to God for His praise. When St. Paul declares that "no one understands" the speaker, for he "utters mysteries in the Spirit", we may be justified in taking "no one" in an absolutely universal sense: that is, there is no earthly language (whether past or present) containing the words spoken in this manner. This tentative exegesis would therefore transport us beyond glossolalia in the strict meaning of the term. We are reminded of the Apostle's assertion in Romans 8:26 about the Holy Spirit's intervention in the soul to evoke "sighs" or "groanings" too profound for normal verbal expression. When the mind of the speaker is shut down (so to speak) by these unanalyzable utterances, when mundane intellectual operations are suspended, then, in the quiet of the soul, the Holy Spirit may find His opportunity. Upon the interface of the soul with the Lord and Giver of life, their communion may burst forth in a language of praise that is neither entirely human nor entirely divine, but the fruit or offspring of human love responding to Divine Love. Perhaps this quasi-angelical prayer is a dim foreshadowing of the ecstatic chants that the glorified human vocal cords will trill when the mind of the resurrected person beholds the Divine Essence in the Beatific Vision.

Miracles

It is fitting for the Holy Spirit to confirm the words of prophecy by working wondrous supernatural deeds through the prophet, in order to make the prophetic message more credible (see Mark 16:17-18, 20). St. Thomas cautions us that a true miracle is some marvel that goes beyond the natural capacity of any and all created powers. (Examples would be the resurrection of the body from the dead, the coincident occupation of the same place by two different bodies, and apparitions creating the effect of bilocation.) Hence, God alone can perform a miracle in the strict or unqualified sense; a creature (such as the prophet) can serve at most as an instrumental cause. If a saint (whether in the Old Testament or the New Testament) revived someone who had died, the resuscitation was obviously accomplished solely through divine power. Similarly, the gift of projection of bodily presence or apparent bilocation (seemingly granted to Ven. Mary of Agreda and St.

Padre Pio) would require divine power.

When an angel (whether good or bad) brings about some astonishing physical occurrence, it may appear "miraculous" (taken in a broad or qualified sense) to human beings, but it is simply a result of the natural angelic power to effect local movement in the material universe. (Two examples would be the explosive stirring up of mineral and fiery forces to destroy Sodom and Gomorrah in Genesis 19:13, 21-22, 24-25, and the devastation of Job's family and property in Job 1:12-19. Moreover, the parting of the Red Sea through a continuous "strong wind" in Exodus 14 would certainly have been within the natural sphere of angelic power.)

Angels can also take on various forms by employing a coalescence of environmental elements (from the air or earth). But they do not truly become incarnate, as Christ truly assumed flesh from His mother's body in the hypostatic union. (Two examples of such angelophanies would be the apparition of St. Raphael in the book of Tobit and the apparition of an angel to Gideon in Judges 6.)

Although the astounding feats of angels are not genuine miracles, real physical entities may sometimes be involved (when it is not a question of mere semblances provoked in the human imagination or conjured up in the outer world). Yet the means by which these real things are produced or made present is not due to a conversion of matter, but rather to rapid and invisible changes in the positions of objects -- an extraordinary "sleight of hand". (An example of this might be exhibited when Pharaoh's Egyptian magicians caused to appear actual serpents and frogs by invoking occult demonic power in Exodus 7:12 and 8:7 [8:3 in the *New American Bible*].) When wicked human beings (such as the Antichrist) perform prodigies, they are done either through diabolical agency or through sophisticated illusions (probably utilizing advanced radio-electronic technology), in order to deceive the unwary.

True miracles, enacted by divine power, are always for the good of mankind. God works them through the secondary causality of angels or men for one of two reasons. The first purpose is to confirm the truth of a proclamation. (Two examples are the proper worship of the one God confirmed by the miracle of fire at Elijah's command in 1 Kings 18:36-39 and the warning messages of our Lady confirmed by the gyration and spinning descent of the sun at Fatima.) The second purpose is to attest to the holiness of a person as a model of virtue. (Examples are the miracles of Elijah and Elisha in 1 Kings 17 and 2 Kings 4-5, the miracles of St. Paul alluded to in Acts 19:11-12, the miracles attributed to St. Anthony of Padua, St. Thérèse of Lisieux, St. Padre Pio -- and in fact the miracles required for the canonization of any saint.) For the first reason God can use anyone (good or bad) as a channel of miracles, because what is at stake is not the sanctity of the doer but rather the veracity of the doctrine preached in the name of God. (See Matthew 7:21-23.) But obviously the second reason applies only to people whose lives radiate sanctity.

Aquinas deals at greater length with miracles, especially healing, in his other masterpiece, the *Summa contra Gentiles* (Book III-II, Chapters 101-106). Healing is an important kind of miracle, because health is normally an intimate and intense desire of human beings. A restoration to sound physical health may be miraculous in one of two ways. First, in a lesser way, a cure need not be beyond the power of natural causes considered in their absolute totality, but it may be beyond their power according to the manner in which the cure occurs: for example, the sudden vanishing of some illness or traumatic injury from which recovery normally takes a significant duration of time, or the even more awesome instantaneous healing of severe disability, chronic disease, or fatal sickness. Second, in a greater way, a cure may utterly transcend all creaturely power: for example, the restoration to life of someone who has evidently died (as in 1 Kings 17:17-24, Mark 5:35-42, Luke 7:11-17, and Acts 9:36-41). It may be argued, though, that some of the cures of disease and disability wrought by Jesus and the Apostles through divine power are possibly within the bounds of natural angelic power (for example, certain cases of hemorrhage or even blindness and lameness). Even here, however, the good angels would never endow mankind with such benefits without divine permission and cooperation. But, so long as it is God's will, who cares whether a cure comes directly from Christ, or from Him through the intermediation of an angel, a saint, or a human person on earth? Beggars can't be choosers, and the bottom-line is the same. If you're hurting, a cure is a cure ... right?

✝

Appendix 3
Poem in Tribute to Frank Kelly
(by Heidi Maloney)

My Humble Hero

There are people in this life, who give much more than they will ever know,
They influence your life and shape you by the example that they show.

They nurture you with their love and inspire you in the simple things they do,
They give freely of themselves; and by doing so they become a part of you.

My gentle friend is one of these people; his love is powerful indeed,
He can lift a wounded spirit and guide you in time of need.

With love he opens his heart to all of those the Lord sends his way,
He inspires a sense of hope; he encourages them and helps them pray.

He walks with a smile and a happy heart, his rosary beads in hand,
A pocketful of prayers he says every day, and wisdom beyond that of man.

He is always helping people in his efforts to share God's love,
Guided not by the world or material things but only by the
holiness above.

He has a selfless, genuine goodness, a generous spirit so
precious and rare,
He always makes the time to listen and pray and takes the
time to care.

In his presence you feel God's comfort and it's the truth you
will receive,
His silent strength comes from the Lord and how deeply he
believes.

His warmth and kindness touch this world and everyone he
meets,
His light-hearted way comforts the lost and all of the people
he greets.

He never complains of his own discomfort and he doesn't let
the world see,
The suffering that affects him everyday for he's human like
you and me.

He prays to the Lord and Mary and he loves all of his heavenly
friends.
They are the source of his love and joy and a wisdom that
never ends.

So blessed be My Humble Hero who is always there to lift those
who fall,
By sharing his faith with others, he has given the most
precious gift of all.

✝
Appendix 4
Prayers

Prayer for Deliverance

Lord Jesus Christ, by faith I turn to you now. I ask You to give me the joy and the peace of knowing You. I want You to come into my life and be my Lord and Savior. I ask You to deliver me from the things of this world that stand between You and me. I need You, Lord Jesus Christ. Fill me with your Holy Spirit that I may live my life as a child of God. I want to be free of my sins, free of the attacks of Satan, and free of sickness. Come, Lord Jesus Christ, be my Lord and Savior. Amen.

Prayer of Offering of Suffering

O Heavenly Father, I come to You today with all my pains and sufferings. I thank You for allowing me to offer these pains and sufferings to You, so that I may come to know your Son Jesus Christ. When offering these gifts of pains and sufferings to You, I thank You for them, because whether they came from my sinfulness or from someone else's sinfulness, I know that through them You allow my pride and jealousy to end. I thank You, Father and Son, because You also allow me to know Mother Mary and the Holy Spirit, the Lord and Giver of Life, so that I can be shown all my sins today, repent and give You glory, and then go on to Life. Amen.

Prayer to Receive the Release of the Holy Spirit

Lord Jesus Christ, I need You. I want to belong to You from now on and never to separate myself from You. I open the door of my life and receive You as my Savior and Lord. I want to realize more fully that You have freed me from the dominion of darkness and the rule of Satan, and I want to enter more fully into Your kingdom as a member of Your Body.

I will turn away from all wrongdoing, and I will avoid everything that leads to wrongdoing. I ask You to forgive me for all my sins. I thank You for Your love and mercy, for forgiving me my sins, and for cleansing me of all unrighteousness. I promise to obey You as my Lord.

I offer my life to You, and I ask You to transform me into the person You want me to be.

Lord God, I thank You for coming to dwell with me when I was baptized as a child, and for pouring out Your Holy Spirit on me when I was confirmed as a youth. I now ask You to help me open myself up completely to the action of the Holy Spirit, so that the fullness of Your all-powerful healing love may penetrate to the depths of my being and be faithfully released in my life.

Amen.